Blockchain

for
dummies®
A Wiley Brand

Blockchain

2nd Edition

by Tiana Laurence

A Wiley Brand

Blockchain For Dummies®, 2nd Edition

Published by: **John Wiley & Sons, Inc.**, 111 River Street, Hoboken, NJ 07030-5774, www.wiley.com

Copyright © 2019 by John Wiley & Sons, Inc., Hoboken, New Jersey

Published simultaneously in Canada

For general information on our other products and services, please contact our Customer Care Department within the U.S. at 877-762-2974, outside the U.S. at 317-572-3993, or fax 317-572-4002. For technical support, please visit https://hub.wiley.com/community/support/dummies.

Wiley publishes in a variety of print and electronic formats and by print-on-demand. Some material included with standard print versions of this book may not be included in e-books or in print-on-demand. If this book refers to media such as a CD or DVD that is not included in the version you purchased, you may download this material at http://booksupport.wiley.com. For more information about Wiley products, visit www.wiley.com.

Library of Congress Control Number: 2019936497

ISBN 978-1-119-55501-8 (pbk); ISBN 978-1-119-55517-9 (ebk); ISBN 978-1-119-55513-1 (ebk)

Manufactured in the United States of America

C10009021_032219

Contents at a Glance

Table of Contents

Introduction

Welcome to *Blockchain For Dummies!* If you want to find out what blockchains are and the basics of how to use them, this is the book for you. Many people think blockchains are difficult to understand. They might also think that blockchains are just about cryptocurrencies like Bitcoin, but they're are so much more. Anyone can master the basics of blockchains.

In this book, you find helpful advice for navigating the blockchain world and cryptocurrencies that run them. You also find practical step-by-step tutorials that will build your understanding of how blockchains work and where they add value. You don't need a background in programming, economics, or world affairs to understand this book, but I do touch on all these subjects because blockchain technology intersects all of them.

About This Book

This book explains the basics of blockchains, smart contracts, and cryptocurrencies. You probably picked up this book because you've heard about blockchains, know they're important, but have no idea what they are, how they work, or why you should care. This book answers all these questions in easy-to-understand terms.

This book is a bit different than just about any other blockchain book on the market. It provides a survey of all the key blockchains in the public market, how they work, what they do, and something useful you can try with them today.

This book also covers the landscape of blockchain technology and points out some of the key things to be aware of for your own blockchain projects. Here, you find out how to install an Ethereum wallet, create and execute a smart contract, make entries into Bitcoin and Factom, and earn cryptocurrencies.

You don't have to read the book cover to cover. Just flip to the subject that you're interested in.

Finally, within this book, you may note that some web addresses break across two lines of text. If you're reading this book in print and want to visit one of these web pages, simply key in the web address exactly as it's noted in the text, pretending as though the line break doesn't exist. If you're reading this as an e-book, you've got it easy — just click the web address to be taken directly to the web page.

Foolish Assumptions

I don't make many assumptions about you and your experience with cryptocurrency, programing, and legal matters but I do assume the following:

>> You have a computer, a smartphone, and access to the Internet.

>> You know the basics of how to use your computer and the Internet.

>> You know how to navigate through menus within programs.

>> You're new to blockchain and you aren't a skilled programmer. Of course, if you are a skilled programmer, you can still get a lot out of this book — you just may be able to breeze past some of the step-by-step guidelines.

Icons Used in This Book

Throughout this book, I use icons in the margin to draw your attention to certain kinds of information. Here's what the icons mean:

TIP

The Tip icon marks tips and shortcuts that you can use to make blockchains easier to use.

REMEMBER

The Remember icon marks the information that's especially important to know — the stuff you'll want to commit to memory. To siphon off the most important information in each chapter, just skim through these icons.

TECHNICAL
STUFF

The Technical Stuff icon marks information of a highly technical nature that you can skip over without missing the main point of the subject at hand.

WARNING

The Warning icon tells you to watch out! It marks important information that may save you headaches — or tokens.

Beyond the Book

In addition to the material in the print or e-book you're reading right now, this product also comes with some access-anywhere goodies on the web. Check out the free Cheat Sheet for more on blockchains. To get this Cheat Sheet, simply go to www.dummies.com and type **Blockchain For Dummies Cheat Sheet** in the Search box.

Where to Go from Here

You can apply blockchain technology to virtually every business domain. Right now there is explosive growth in financial, healthcare, government, insurance industries, and this is just the beginning. The whole world is changing and the possibilities are endless.

1
Getting Started with Blockchain

Chapter **1**

Introducing Blockchain

O riginally, *blockchain* was just the computer science term for how to struc-ture and share data. Today blockchains are hailed the "fifth evolution" of computing.

Blockchains are a novel approach to the distributed database. The innovation comes from incorporating old technology in new ways. You can think of block-chains as distributed databases that a group of individuals controls and that store and share information.

There are many different types of blockchains and blockchain applications. Block-chain is an all-encompassing technology that is integrating across platforms and hardware all over the world.

Beginning at the Beginning: What Blockchains Are

A blockchain is a data structure that makes it possible to create a digital ledger of data and share it among a network of independent parties. There are many differ-ent types of blockchains.

- » **Public blockchains:** Public blockchains, such as Bitcoin, are large distributed networks that are run through a native cryptocurrency. A *cryptocurrency* is a unique bit of data that that can be traded between two parties. Public blockchains are open for anyone to participate at any level and have open-source code that their community maintains.

- » **Permissioned blockchains:** Permissioned blockchains, such as Ripple, control roles that individuals can play within the network. They're still large and distributed systems that use a native token. Their core code may or may not be open source.

- » **Private blockchains:** Private blockchains also known as distributed ledger technology (DLT) tend to be smaller and do not utilize a token or cryptocurrency. Their membership is closely controlled. These types of blockchains are favored by consortiums that have trusted members and trade confidential information.

All three types of blockchains use cryptography to allow each participant on any given network to manage the ledger in a secure way without the need for a central authority to enforce the rules. The removal of central authority from the database structure is one of the most important and powerful aspects of blockchains.

REMEMBER

Blockchains create permanent records and histories of transactions, but nothing is really permanent. The permanence of the record is based on the dependability and health of the network. In the context of blockchains, this means that if a large portion of the blockchain community wanted to change information written to their blockchain, they could. Cryptocurrency is used as a reward to incentivize lots of users to facilitate the healthy function of the network through competition. If the records are changed inappropriately, this is known as a 51 percent attack. Small networks with few independent minors are vulnerable because it doesn't take much effort to change their information, and powerful miners could do so and gain extra cryptocurrency. Ethereum Class experienced just this type of attack.

When data is recorded in a blockchain, it's extremely difficult to change or remove it. When someone wants to add a record to a blockchain, also called a *transaction* or an *entry*, users in the network who have validation control verify the proposed transaction. This is where things get tricky because every blockchain has a slightly different spin on how this works and who can validate a transaction.

What blockchains do

A blockchain is a peer-to-peer system with no central authority managing data flow. One of the key ways to removing central control while maintaining data integrity is to have a large distributed network of independent users. This means that the computers that make up the network are in more than one location. These computers are often referred to as *full nodes*.

Figure 1-1 shows a visualization of the structure of the Bitcoin blockchain network. You can see it in action at `http://dailyblockchain.github.io`.

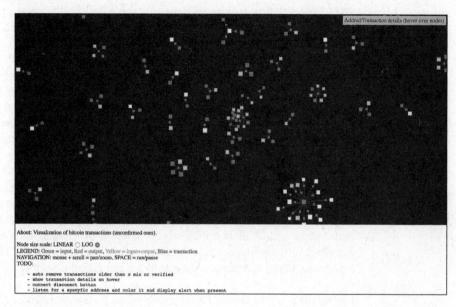

FIGURE 1-1:
The structure of the Bitcoin blockchain network.

To prevent the network from being corrupted, not only are blockchains decentralized but they often also utilize a cryptocurrency. Blockchain networks produce cryptocurrencies as an incentive to maintain the integrity of the network. Many cryptocurrencies are traded on exchanges like stocks.

Cryptocurrencies work a little differently on each blockchain. Basically, the software pays the hardware to operate. The software is the blockchain protocol. Well-known blockchain protocols include Bitcoin, Ethereum, Ripple, Bitcoin Cash, Stellar, and EOS. The hardware consists of the full nodes that are securing the data in the network.

Why blockchains matter

Blockchains are recognized as the "fifth evolution" of computing because they're a new trust layer for the Internet. Before blockchains, trust was established by central authorities that would issue certificates. One you may be familiar with is Secure Sockets Layer (SSL) client certificates. An SSL certificate is the "green lock" that is next to a web domain. It lets you know you're on a secure website.

SSL certificates have proven to not be foolproof. Certificates have been stolen from the domains of the Central Intelligence Agency (CIA), the U.K.'s Secret Intelligence Service (commonly known as MI6), Microsoft, Yahoo!, Skype, Facebook, and Twitter. Relying on a third party allows for a single point of failure.

Blockchains, on the other hand, establish trust in novel ways. Proof-of-work (POW) blockchains require miners to have a full and accurate history of their transactions to participate on the network. Proof-of-stake (POS) blockchains create trust by requiring nodes that are processing transactions to "stake" some cryptocurrency that may be forfeited if they're caught defrauding the network. Private blockchains build confidence by distributing data across a network of connected but independent participants that are known by each other and can be held accountable. Each type of blockchain uses different incentive systems to establish trust that each participant in the network will cooperate in keeping a full and unaltered history of each transaction or entry that is made within the database they share.

When data is permanent and reliable in a digital format, you can transact business online in ways that, in the past, were only possible offline. Everything that has stayed analog, including property rights and identity, can now be created and maintained online. Slow business and banking processes, such as money wires and fund settlements, can now be done nearly instantaneously. The implications for secure digital records are enormous for the global economy.

Blockchains are important because they allow for new efficiency and reliability in the exchange of valuable and private information that once required a third party to facilitate, such as the movement of money and the authenticity of identity. This is a big deal because much of our society and economy has been structured around establishing trust, enforcing trust when it's broken, and third parties that facilitate trust. You can imagine how this simple software can be utilized to fix areas that have proven to not be foolproof, such as voting, supply chain management, money movement, and the exchange of property.

The Structure of Blockchains

Each blockchain is structured slightly differently. However, Bitcoin is a great blockchain to study because it was used as a template for most subsequent blockchains. The data on Bitcoin is structured so that each full *node* (the computers running the network) contains all the data in the network. This model is compelling from a data persistence point of view. It ensures that the data will stay intact even if a few of the nodes become compromised. However, because every node has a full copy of the history of transactions, since the very beginning, and every transaction in the future, it requires that the entries be as small as possible from a storage capacity point of view.

Comparatively, other distributed networks you may have heard of like Napster and Pirate Bay are an online index of data. Individual files are shared from specific nodes in the network. This allows sharing of large files. However, because the data you may be interested in is not available on all the participants in the network, obtaining the data you're interested in is problematic. It's also difficult to know if the data that you're pulling down is intact and has not be corrupted or contains information you don't want, such as a virus.

The way that Bitcoin coordinates the organization and input of new data comprises three core elements:

>> **Block:** A list of transactions recorded into a ledger over a given period. The size, period, and triggering event for blocks is different for every blockchain.

Not all blockchains are recording and securing a record of the movement of their cryptocurrency as their primary objective. But all blockchain do record the movement of their cryptocurrency or token. Think of the *transaction* as simply being the recording of data. Assigning a value to it (such as happens in a financial transaction) is used to interpret what that data means.

>> **Chain:** A hash that links one block to another, mathematically "chaining" them together. This is one of the most difficult concepts in blockchain to comprehend. It's also the magic that glues blockchains together and allows them to create mathematical trust.

The hash in blockchain is created from the data that was in the previous block. The hash is a fingerprint of this data and locks blocks in order and time.

TECHNICAL STUFF

Although blockchains are a relatively new innovation, hashing is not. Hashing was invented over 30 years ago. This old innovation is being used because it creates a one-way function that cannot be decrypted. A hashing function creates a mathematical algorithm that maps data of any size to a bit string of a fixed size. A bit string is usually 32 characters long, which then represents the data that was hashed. The Secure Hash Algorithm (SHA) is one of some cryptographic hash functions used in blockchains. SHA-256 is a common algorithm that generates an almost-unique, fixed-size 256-bit (32-byte) hash. For practical purposes, think of a hash as a digital fingerprint of data that is used to lock it in place within the blockchain.

>> **Network:** The network is composed of "full nodes." Think of them as the computer running an algorithm that is securing the network. Each node contains a complete record of all the transactions that were ever recorded in that blockchain.

The nodes are located all over the world and can be operated by anyone. It's difficult, expensive, and time-consuming to operate a full node, so people don't do it for free. They're incentivized to operate a node because they want to earn cryptocurrency. The underlying blockchain algorithm rewards them for their service. The reward is usually a token or cryptocurrency, like Bitcoin.

TIP

The terms *Bitcoin* and *blockchain* are often used interchangeably, but they're not the same. Bitcoin has a blockchain. The Bitcoin blockchain is the underlying protocol that enables the secure transfer of Bitcoin. The term *Bitcoin* is the name of the cryptocurrency that powers the Bitcoin network. The blockchain is a class of software, and Bitcoin is a specific cryptocurrency.

Blockchain Applications

Blockchain applications are built around the idea that network is the arbitrator. This type of system is an unforgiving and blind environment. Computer code becomes law, and rules are executed as they were written and interpreted by the network. Computers don't have the same social biases and behaviors as humans do.

The network can't interpret intent (at least not yet). Insurance contracts arbitrated on a blockchain have been heavily investigated as a use case built around this idea.

Another interesting thing that blockchains enable is impeccable record keeping. They can be used to create a clear timeline of who did what and when. Many industries and regulatory bodies spend countless hours trying to asses this problem. Blockchain-enabled record keeping will relieve some of the burdens that are created when we try to interpret the past.

The Blockchain Life Cycle

Blockchains originated with the creation of Bitcoin. It demonstrated that a group of individuals who had never met could operate online within a system that was desensitized to cheat others that were cooperating on the network.

The original Bitcoin network was built to secure the Bitcoin cryptocurrency. It has around 5,000 full nodes and is globally distributed. It's primarily used to trade Bitcoin and exchange value, but the community saw the potential of doing a lot more with the network. Because of its size and time-tested security, it's also being used to secure other smaller blockchains and blockchain applications.

The Ethereum network is a second evolution of the blockchain concept. It takes the traditional blockchain structure and adds several new programming languages that are built inside of it. Like Bitcoin, it has over 10,000 full nodes and is globally distributed. Ethereum is primarily used to trade Ether and create smart contracts. The most popular Ethereum smart contract is the ERC 20. It allows for the generation of interchangeable tokens. These tokens can be used for fundraising purposes. You can discover more about smart contracts in Chapter 5.

There is a third evolution in blockchain technology that is under active development addressing speed and data size constraints. Fixing these issues will enable blockchain technology to be used more realistically with mainstream applications. It will take several years before it is clear what structure will win out.

Popular new developments include *sharding*, a type of database partitioning that separates large databases into smaller parts called *data shards*. An Ethereum development effort called *fork choice rule* splits the Ethereum blockchain into several parallel networks. It may allow Ethereum to scale more efficiently and reduce the congestion on the network, increasing transaction speeds and lowering transaction costs.

Another popular scaling theory is called POS. I cover this subject in more detail in Chapter 8. Broadly, POS is the concept of putting up tokens or cryptocurrency as a bond for processing transactions. If the node is corrupted and does not process the transactions accurately, the node may forfeit their tokens or cryptocurrency.

A third effort to scale blockchain technology utilizes trusted nodes. For example, the Factom network operates with federated nodes and an unlimited number of auditing nodes. These nodes are trusted with ensuring the system. Factom's elected network is small, just over 60 nodes. To hedge for security risks, Factom anchors itself into other distributed networks to piggyback on the security of more extensive systems. Factom also partitions its network into smaller, faster, more easily managed parts called *chains*. Factom has faster transaction speeds and lower transaction costs than POW blockchains.

Consensus: The Driving Force of Blockchains

Blockchains are powerful tools because they create honest systems that self-correct without the need of a third party to enforce the rules. They accomplish the enforcement of rules through their consensus algorithm.

In the blockchain world, *consensus* is the process of developing an agreement among a group of commonly mistrusting shareholders. These are the full nodes on the network. The full nodes are validating transactions that are entered into the network to be recorded as part of the ledger.

Figure 1-2 shows the concept of how blockchains come to agreement.

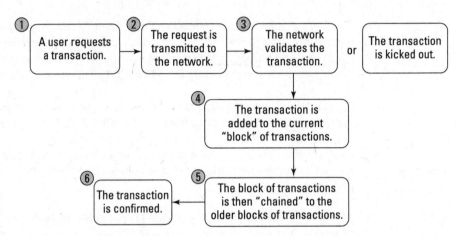

FIGURE 1-2:
How blockchains
work.

Each blockchain has its own algorithms for creating agreement within its network on the entries being added. There are many different models for creating consensus because each blockchain is creating different kinds of entries. Some blockchains are trading value, others are storing data, and others are securing systems and contracts.

Bitcoin, for example, is trading the value of its token between members on its network. The tokens have a market value, so the requirements related to performance, scalability, consistency, threat model, and failure model will be higher. Bitcoin operates under the assumption that a malicious attacker may want to corrupt the history of trades in order to steal tokens. Bitcoin prevents this from happening by using a consensus model called "proof of work" that solves the Byzantine general's problem: "How do you know that the information you are looking at has not been changed internally or externally?" Because changing or manipulating data is almost always possible, the reliability of data is a big problem for computer science.

Most blockchains operate under the premise that they will be attacked by outside forces or by users of the system. The expected threat and the degree of trust that the network has in the nodes that operate the blockchain will determine the type of consensus algorithm that they use to settle their ledger. For example, Bitcoin and Ethereum expect a very high degree of threat and use a strong consensus algorithm called *proof of work*. There is no trust in the network.

On the other end of the spectrum, blockchains that are used to record financial transactions between known parties can use a lighter and faster consensus. Their need for high-speed transactions is more important. Proof of work is too slow and costly for them to operate because of the comparatively few participants within the network and immediate finality need for each transaction. They also do not need a token or cryptocurrency to incentivize transaction processing. So, they eliminate these things from their system and run faster and cheaper than POW systems.

Blockchains in Use

Thousands of blockchains and blockchain applications are in existence today. The whole world has become obsessed with the ideas of moving money faster, incorporating and governing in a distributed network, and building secure applications and hardware.

You can see many of these public blockchains by going to a cryptocurrency exchange.

Figure 1-3 shows the altcoin exchange for Poloniex (https://poloniex.com), a cryptocurrency trading platform.

FIGURE 1-3: The altcoin exchange platform.

Blockchains are moving beyond the trading value market and are being incorporated into all sorts of industries. Blockchains add a new trust layer that now makes working online secure in a way that was not possible beforehand.

Current blockchain uses

Most up-and-running blockchain applications revolve around moving money or other forms of value quickly and cheaply. This includes trading public company stock, paying employees in other countries, and exchanging one currency for another.

Blockchains are also now being used as part of a software security stack. The U.S. Department of Homeland Security has been investigating blockchain software that secures Internet of Things (IoT) devices. The IoT world has some of the most to gain from this innovation, because it's especially vulnerable to spoofing and other forms of hacking. IoT devices have also become more pervasive, and security has become more reliant on them. Hospital systems, self-driving cars, and safety systems are prime examples.

Initial Coin Offerings (ICOs) are another exciting blockchain innovation. They're a type of smart contract that allows the issuer to offer a token in exchange for investment funds. Often used as a non-dilutive fundraising option, entrepreneurs globally have raised billions of dollars. Governments and regulators have been quick to crack down on ICOs. The tokens may be unlicensed securities, and the offering may be defrauding investors. The technology is impressive even if compliance issues are still being addressed.

One of the fantastic innovations inherent in ICO tokens is that they're a self-clearing and self-settling instrument. In our current system for trading securities, there are two types of clearing agencies: clearing corporations and depositories. Clearing corporations audit transactions and act as intermediaries in making settlements. Depositories hold securities certificates and maintain ownership records of the securities. Blockchains perform both these functions for tokens without needing third parties to audit and retain possession of the assets. You can learn more about ICO tokens in Chapter 5.

Future blockchain applications

Larger and longer-run blockchain projects that are being explored now include government-backed land record systems, identity, and international travel security applications.

The possibilities of a blockchain-infused future have excited the imaginations of business people, governments, political groups, and humanitarians across the world. Countries such as the UK, Singapore, and the United Arab Emirates see it as a way to cut cost, create new financial instruments, and keep clean records. They have active investments and initiatives exploring blockchain.

Blockchains have laid a foundation where the need for trust has been taken out of the equation. Where before asking for "trust" was a big deal, with blockchains it's small. Also, the infrastructure that enforces the rule if that trust is broken can be lighter. Much of society is built on trust and enforcement of rules. The social and economic implications of blockchain applications can be emotionally and politically polarizing because blockchain will change how we structure value-based and socially based transactions.

Chapter **2**

Picking a Blockchain

The blockchain industry is complex and growing in size and capabilities every day. When you understand the three core types of blockchains and their limitations, you'll know what's possible with this new technology.

This chapter is all about assessing blockchain technology and developing a project plan. It puts the following chapters about individual blockchain platforms and applications into context.

Here, you see how to assess the three different types of blockchain platforms, what's being built on each type, and why. I give you a few tools that help you outline your project, predict obstacles, and overcome challenges.

Where Blockchains Add Substance

There's a lot of buzz surrounding blockchains and the cryptocurrencies that run them. Some of this buzz just stems from the fluctuation in the value of cryptocurrencies and the fear that blockchain technology will disrupt many industry and government functions. A lot of money has poured into research and development because stakeholders don't want to be made obsolete and entrepreneurs want to explore new business models.

When it comes to finding an opportunity for blockchain technology to add value to an organization, often the question arises, "Where do blockchains add value and how are they different from existing technologies?"

Blockchains are a special type of database. They can be utilized anywhere you would use a normal database — but it may not make sense to go through the trouble and expense of using a blockchain when a normal database can do the job.

You really see value in using some form of a blockchain when you want to share information with parties you don't fully truest, your data needs to be audited, or your data is at risk of being compromised internally or externally. None of these questions are simple, and the correct solutions can be difficult to ascertain.

This section helps narrow down your options.

Determining your needs

Blockchains come in a lot of flavors. You'll find one that matches your needs — the trick is finding it! Mapping your needs to the best blockchain can be overwhelming. Whenever I have lots of options and often conflicting needs, I like to utilize a weighted decision matrix.

A weighted decision matrix is an excellent tool for evaluating the needs of a project and then mapping those needs to possible solutions. The key advantage of the matrix is to help you quantify and prioritize individual needs for your project and simplify decision making. Weighted decision matrixes also prevent you from becoming overwhelmed by individual criteria. If done properly, this tool allows you to converge on single idea that is compatible with all your goals.

To create a weighted decision matrix, follow these steps:

1. **Brainstorm the key criteria or goals that your team needs to meet.**

TIP

If you aren't sure of the criteria you need to consider when evaluating your blockchain project, here are a few things to keep in mind:

- Scale and volume
- Speed and latency
- Security and immutability
- Storage capacity and structural needs

Your team will have its own list of objects and priorities. These are just a few to consider while evaluating the correct platform to use to meet your needs.

2. **Reduce the list of criteria to no more than ten items.**

   If you're having a hard time refining your list of needs, consider using a comparison matrix tool.

3. **Create a table in Microsoft Excel or a similar program.**

4. **Enter the design criteria in the first column.**

5. **Assign a relative weight to each criterion based on how important that objective is to the success of the project.**

   Limit the number of points to 10 and distribute them between all your criteria — for example, 1 = low, 2 = medium, and 3 = high priority.

   If you're working in a team, have each member weight the criteria separately.

6. **Add up the numbers for each objective and divide by the number of team members for a composite team weight.**

7. **Make any needed adjustment to weights to make sure each criteria are weighted correctly.**

Congratulations! You now have a ranked list of criteria you need to meet to be successful with your blockchain project.

Defining your goal

You can easily get lost building a blockchain project that doesn't have a clear goal or purpose. Take the time to understand where you and your team would like to go and what the final objective is. For example, a goal might be to trade an asset with a partner company with no intermediary. This is a big goal with many stakeholders.

Build back to a small project that is a minimal viable use case for the technology that clearly articulates added value or savings for your company. Along the same lines as the earlier example, a smaller goal would be to build a private network that can exchange value between trusted parties.

Then build on that value. The next win might be building an instrument that is tradable on your new platform. Each step should demonstrate a small win and value created.

Choosing a Solution

There are three core types of blockchains: public networks like Bitcoin, permissioned networks such as Ripple, and private ones like Hijro.

Blockchains do a few straightforward things:

>> They move value and trade value quickly and at a very low cost.

>> They create nearly permanent data histories.

Blockchain technology also allows for a few less-straightforward solutions such as the ability to prove that you have a "thing" without revealing it to the other party. It is also possible to "prove the negative," or prove what is missing within a dataset or system. This feature is particularly useful for auditing and proving compliance.

Table 2-1 lists common uses cases that are suited for each type of blockchain.

TABLE 2-1　　**Table Head**

Primary Purpose	Type of Blockchain
Move value between untrusted parties	Public
Move value between trusted parties	Private
Trade value between unlike things	Permissioned
Trade value of the same thing	Public
Create decentralized organization	Public or permissioned
Create decentralized contract	Public or permissioned
Trade securitized assets	Public or permissioned
Build identity for people or things	Public
Publish for public recordkeeping	Public
Publish for private recordkeeping	Public or permissioned
Preform auditing of records or systems	Public or permissioned
Publish land title data	Public
Trade digital money or assets	Public or permissioned
Create systems for Internet of Things (IoT) security	Public
Build systems security	Public

There may be exceptions depending on your project, and it is possible to use a different type of blockchain to reach your goal. But in general, here is how to break down different types of networks and understand their strengths and weaknesses:

>> **Public networks** are large and decentralized, anyone can participate within them at any level — this includes things like running a full node, mining cryptocurrency, trading tokens, or publishing entries. They tend to be more secure and immutable then private or permissioned networks. They're often slower and more expensive to use. They're are secured with a cryptocurrency and have limited storage capacity.

>> **Permissioned networks** are viewable to the public, but participation is controlled. Many of them utilize a cryptocurrency, but they can have a lower cost for applications that are built on top of them. This feature makes it easier to scale project and increase transaction volume. Permissioned networks can be very fast with low latency and have higher storage capacity over public networks.

>> **Private networks** are shared between trusted parties and may not be viewable to the public. They're very fast and may have no latency. They also have a low cost to run and can be built in an industrious weekend. Most private networks do not utilize a cryptocurrency and do not have the same immutability and security of decentralized networks. Storage capacity may be unlimited.

There are also hybrids between these three core types of blockchains that seek to find the right balance of security, auditability, scalability, and data storage for applications built on top of them.

Drawing a blockchain decision tree

Some of the decisions you face while working on a blockchain project within your organization can be difficult and challenging. It pays to take time making decisions that involve

>> **Uncertainty:** Many of the facts around blockchain technology may be unknown and untested.

>> **Complexity:** Blockchains have many interrelated factors to consider.

>> **High-risk consequences:** The impact of the decision may be significant to your organization.

>> **Alternatives:** There may be alternative technologies and types of blockchains, each with its own set of uncertainties and consequences.

>> **Interpersonal issues:** You need to understand how blockchain technology could affect different people within your organization.

A decision tree is a useful support tool that will help you uncover consequences, event outcomes, resource costs, and utility of developing a blockchain project.

You can draw decision trees on paper or use a computer application. Here are the steps to create one for uncovering other challenges around your project:

TIP

1. **Get a large sheet of paper.**

   The more choices there are, and the more complicated the decision, the bigger the sheet of paper you'll need.

2. **Draw a square on the left side of the paper.**

3. **Write a description of the core goal and criteria for your project in that square.**

4. **Draw lines to the right of the square for each issue.**

5. **Write a description of each issue along each line.**

   Assign a probability value to encounter each issue.

TIP

6. **Brainstorm solutions for each issue.**

7. **Write a description of each solution along each line.**

8. **Continue this process until you've explored each issue and discovered a possible solution for each.**

Have teammates challenge and review all your issues and solutions before finalizing it.

Making a plan

At this point, you should have a clear understanding of your goals, obstacles, and what blockchain options you have available.

Here's a simple road map for building your project:

1. **Explain the project to key stakeholders and discuss its key components and foreseen outcomes.**

2. **Write up a project plan.**

   This is a living set of documents that will change over the life of your project.

3. **Develop the performance measurements, scope statement, schedule, and cost baselines.**

4. **Consider creating a risk management plan and a staffing plan.**

5. **Get buy-in and define roles and responsibilities.**

6. **Hold a kickoff meeting to begin the project.**

   The meeting should cover the following:

   - Vision for the project
   - Project strategy
   - Project timeline
   - Roles and responsibilities
   - Team-building activities
   - Team commitments
   - How your team will make decisions
   - Key metrics the project will be measured against

REMEMBER

After you complete your project, you aren't done! Go back and analyze your successes and failures. Here are some questions to ask yourself:

>> Are my key stakeholders happy?

>> Did the project stay on schedule?

>> If not, what caused it to be delayed?

>> What did I learn from this project?

>> What do I wish I had done differently?

>> Did I actually create new value for my company or save money?

TIP

You may want to return to this chapter when you have a deeper knowledge of blockchain technology and you're developing a plan to build a project.

Chapter **3**

Getting Your Hands on Blockchain

Blockchains are very powerful tools and are positioned to change how the world moves money, secures systems, and builds digital identities. If you aren't a core developer, you probably won't be doing any in-depth blockchain development in the near future. That said, you still need to understand how blockchains work and what their core limitations are because they'll be integrated into many everyday online interactions in the near future — from how businesses pay people to how governments know that their systems and data are intact and secure.

In this chapter, you dive right into blockchain technology. You purchase your first cryptocurrency and learn how to exchange it for other currencies. You set up special applications that will give you access to a whole ecosystem of decentralized applications (known as Dapps). You also set up a secure environment to use your cryptocurrency. In this chapter, you also create and lease out digital blockchain assets through a blockchain game.

After working through this chapter, you'll understand many of the basic functionalities that blockchain technology offer. You'll also have a basic understanding of some of the additional security you need to have while working with cryptocurrency. This chapter also helps you establish the basic crypto accounts that you need in later chapters.

Diving into Blockchain Technology

The Ethereum blockchain is one of the largest and most powerful blockchains in the world. It was designed to build Dapps, which are applications that are built within a trustless decentralized network. Within the Ethereum network, developers utilize smart contracts to build these applications. Ethereum also utilizes a cryptocurrency called Ether to reward users for providing computing power and creating the trustless system that these smart contracts need to execute.

Smart contracts are not really like a contract you may have seen for a business. Instead, smart contracts are code deployed across a decentralized network. Like a business contract, they have predefined terms. A key difference is that smart contracts are enforced by their blockchain network. They're an important computing innovation because they allow individuals who don't know or trust one another to collaborate without fear that the other party won't perform as outlined by the terms that the two parties have agreed on.

Blockchains that utilize a cryptocurrency can sometimes be called "trustless" systems because the code is enforced by the network (as opposed to a business contract, which is enforced by a court system).

In the following sections, you set up accounts to purchase your first Bitcoin. You also exchange some of the Bitcoin you buy for Ether so you can utilize Ethereum Dapps in the following sections.

Creating a secure environment

The first thing you need to do is create a secure environment to work online. There are a growing number of reasons for you to think about using a secure browser and a virtual private network (VPN). They prevent your data from being collected without your consent and help to avoid hackers. The average user can be targeted by hackers when using cryptocurrency and an unsecured Internet connection.

In this section, you download the Brave web browser, ProtonVPN, and a MetaMask browser extension. You can use all three of these services without paying. However, they also offer improved service for a fee.

Get a piece of paper and pen ready to write down important information. Never take a screenshot or photo of things like passwords or seed phrases.

Downloading and installing the Brave browser

Brave is a new Google Chromium–based secure web browser that is fast, open source, and privacy focused. It blocks advertisements, trackers, and has a feature that lets you reward publishers you like with tokens. Internet pioneer Brendan Eich created Brave; he invented JavaScript and co-founded Mozilla, too.

To download the Brave web browser, follow these steps:

1. **Go to** https://brave.com.
2. **Click Download Brave.**
3. **Go to your downloads folder.**
4. **Double click the Brave browser file.**
5. **Drag and drop the new Brave browser icon to your applications folder.**

Now that you have a more secure web browser, you can add the blockchain extension to it that allows you to explore decentralized applications.

Downloading and installing ProtonVPN

ProtonVPN is a VPN run by a Swiss company. When you use ProtonVPN to browse the web, your Internet connection is encrypted so any would-be attackers can't eavesdrop on your activity. It also allows you to access websites that may be blocked.

To download ProtonVPN, follow these steps:

1. **Go to** https://protonvpn.com.
2. **Click Get ProtonVPN Now.**
3. **Click Get Free.**
4. **Enter your email address when prompted.**

To install ProtonVPN, follow these steps:

1. **Go to your download folder on Mac or PC.**
2. **Double-click the ProtonVPN file.**
3. **Drag and drop the new ProtonVPN icon to your applications folder.**

A VPN is a good second layer of security to help make sure that your connection is secure. To learn more about how you can protect yourself and your devices check out *Cybersecurity For Dummies* by Joseph Steinberg (Wiley).

Downloading, installing, and securing MetaMask

MetaMask is a browser extension that allows you to run Ethereum Dapps right in your browser without running a full Ethereum node. (Ethereum is one of the largest blockchains in the world; see Chapter 5 for more information). MetaMask includes a secure identity vault. It allows you to log into websites, manage your identities on the web, and sign blockchain transactions. You can also keep some Ether cryptocurrency in your MetaMask wallet to make payments online.

To download and install MetaMask, follow these steps:

1. **Open the Brave web browser.**

   See "Downloading and installing the Brave browser," earlier in this chapter if you haven't installed it already.

2. **Go to** https://metamask.io.

3. **Click Get Chrome Extension.**

4. **Click Add to Chrome.**

5. **Click Add Extension inside the pop-up window.**

   You should now see a small fox icon in the upper-right corner of your Brave browser.

Because MetaMask is a wallet, you'll also need to secure and back up your wallet with a strong password and secure your backup seed. A backup seed allows you to recover your wallet if you lose your password.

Grab a pen and notebook or a piece of paper that you can keep private. Then follow these steps:

1. **At the top of your piece of paper, write "MetaMask," "Brave browser," the date, and the device you've download it on.**

2. **Open the Brave web browser.**

3. **Click the fox icon in the upper-right corner.**

4. **Click Continue.**

5. **Create a strong and unique password.**

6. **Write down your username and password.**

7. **Click Create.**

Get another notebook or a separate piece of paper for this next series of steps. (Don't use the same notebook or piece of paper on which you've just written down your username and password.)

1. At the top of your piece of paper, write "MetaMask," "Brave browser," the date, the device you downloaded Brave on, and "Seed phrase."

2. Open the Brave web browser.

3. Click the fox icon on the upper-right corner.

4. Click Accept.

5. Click the lock icon.

6. Write down and number the 12-word phrase.

7. Click Next.

8. Reorder the seed phrase using what you wrote down.

9. Click Done.

TIP

Consider laminating the pieces of paper with your username and password and your backup seed. And remember not to store these two pieces of paper in the same location.

Buying your first Bitcoin

There are several places where you can purchase your first Bitcoin. If you're within the United States, there will be some friction setting up an account and linking it to your credit card or bank account. It may take a day or two for you to be authenticated and allowed to purchase your first cryptocurrency. I recommend using one of the following websites if you're within the United States:

» **Coinbase:** www.coinbase.com

» **Cash App:** https://cash.app

» **Gemini:** https://gemini.com/

» **Robinhood:** https://robinhood.com

Go to one of these sites or another of your choosing and set up an account. You'll want to purchase $10 to $20 worth of cryptocurrency. I suggest purchasing Bitcoin. It's universally accepted and traded for all other cryptocurrencies. You may also have the option to purchase Ether, the Ethereum cryptocurrency used for running Dapps. If so, go ahead and purchase $5 to $10 worth because you'll be using it in the next section. If you're only able to buy Bitcoin, that's okay. You'll be able to trade it for Ether within your wallet using ShapeShift, a low-friction cryptocurrency exchange.

An important note to remember is that cryptocurrency has been in the regulatory gray zone. At the writing of this book, it's possible to purchase and withdraw funds from these sources. Buying and withdrawing cryptocurrency may not be available in the future or within your country or region. If that's the case, you may want to move on to Chapter 5. There, you'll be able to mine on the test net and receive test Ether.

Securing and Exchanging Your Cryptocurrency

If you were able to buy Ether when you set up your account, feel free to skip this section. Here, you'll be setting up a Jaxx wallet to exchange the Bitcoin you bought for Ether using the built-in ShapeShift exchange. The Jaxx wallet was developed by Anthony Di Iorio. He is an early blockchain pioneer and a co-founder of Ethereum.

The device you download the wallet onto can be a computer or phone. For this exercise, you're going to download the Chrome extension. If you choose to download the other wallet types, don't forget that your devices can be compromised. Common cryptocurrency hacking is done through social engineering, like a SIM card hack. You can also lose your assets because you have an insecure Internet connection. Jaxx is considered a hot wallet because it's connected to the Internet, so it has some vulnerabilities.

TIP

There are a few things you can do to help mitigate your risks:

>> Use your VPN.

>> Use Google Authenticator.

>> Use a Google Voice number.

>> Keep a separate email you use only for cryptocurrency accounts.

>> Have a device you use only on a secure connection for your cryptocurrency activities.

>> Never keep any digital records of your passwords and recovery seeds.

Downloading Jaxx

In this section, you will download and set up a cryptocurrency wallet. There are many on the market that help you secure the Bitcoin and other assets that you use. The Jaxx Liberty is a user-friendly wallet that supports more than 80 different cryptocurrencies. It also works great for iOS, Android, desktop, and has a Google Chrome version, too. Feel free to look at other options, too. For example, Exodus. io (`www.exodus.io`) is also another great and easy-to-use wallet.

1. **In your Brave browser, go to** `https://jaxx.io`.
2. **Click Downloads.**
3. **Select Add the Jaxx Liberty Google Chrome Extension to Your Browser.**
4. **Click Add to Chrome.**
5. **Click Add Extension in the popup window.**

Securing your Jaxx wallet

Now you're ready to secure your Jaxx wallet. You'll need at least two clean sheets of paper to write down your seed phrase and password.

REMEMBER

Do not keep your password with your seed phrase.

Follow these steps:

1. **At the top of one sheet of paper, write "Jaxx," "Brave browser," the date, and the device you've downloaded Jaxx on.**
2. **Open the Brave web browser.**
3. **Click the heart icon in the upper-right corner.**
4. **Click Create New Wallet.**
5. **Click I Agree.**
6. **Click Continue.**
7. **Click Back Up Now.**
8. **Select Yes when you see the warning.**
9. **Click Start Backup.**
10. **Write down and number your seed phrase.**
11. **Retype your words in order.**

12. Click Confirm.

13. Click Jaxx Liberty Home.

In the next section, you'll secure a password for your Jaxx wallet for your Brave browser. Don't skip this step — you'll need the password later to access your assets.

Follow these steps:

1. At the top of the second piece of paper, write "Jaxx," "Brave browser," the date, and the device you have downloaded Jaxx on.

2. Open the Brave web browser.

3. Click the heart icon in the upper-right corner.

4. Click the menu icon in your Jaxx wallet.

5. Click Security Password.

6. Select Yes when you see the warning.

7. Click Set Password.

8. Write down a strong unique password on your sheet of paper.

9. Enter your password twice and click Continue.

REMEMBER

Store these two pieces of paper in separate locations. You may want to laminate them just to be safe.

Transferring Bitcoin to Jaxx

In this section, you will add some Bitcoin cryptocurrency to your Jaxx wallet for your Brave browser. Don't skip this step — you'll need the Bitcoin later to buy Ether for the CryptoKitties exercise.

Follow these steps:

1. Open the Brave web browser.

2. Click the heart icon in the upper-right corner.

3. Click Wallets.

4. Click Bitcoin.

5. Click Receive.

6. Click Copy Address.

Trading Bitcoin for Ether

Now you need to open the account in which you keep your Bitcoin. You'll look for a transfer or send button and paste the address into the field when it's presented. After you've received your Bitcoin into your Jaxx wallet, you can use the exchange function. Follow these steps:

1. **Open the Brave web browser.**
2. **Click the heart icon in the upper-right corner.**
3. **Click Wallets.**
4. **Click Bitcoin.**
5. **Click Exchange.**
6. **Under Receive from ShapeShift, select Ethereum ETH.**
7. **Input the amount you would like to exchange.**

   For the next section, you'll need $5 to $10 of Ether.

8. **Click Continue.**
9. **Click connect ShapeShift.**

   You may be prompted to set up a ShapeShift account. If so, go ahead and set one up and take the same precautions you've taken in setting up your Jaxx and MetaMask accounts.

10. **Click Exchange.**

Loading up your MetaMask account

After your exchange has gone through, you can follow the same directions given earlier to send your Ether to your MetaMask account:

1. **Go to the account where you have Ether.**
2. **Click Account.**
3. **Click Send.**
4. **Click the fox icon in the upper-right corner of your browser.**
5. **Click the menu icon.**
6. **Click the Ether address.**

7. Copy the address.

8. Paste your MetaMask Ether address into the Recipient window.

9. Enter the amount you want to send.

10. Click Continue.

11. Click Confirm.

Setting up a CryptoKitties account

In this section, you have a bit of fun using the Ethereum blockchain. Here you learn how to buy a unique blockchain asset, create your very own unique blockchain assets, and then sell your asset on a global market.

This incredibly complex exercise of creating and selling blockchain-based assets is disguised as adorable cat images. Called CryptoKitties, it allows you to collect and create a new digital cat. Each image has unique characteristics that it has inherited from its parent images. When you have "bred" a new CryptoKitty, you can then lease your cat to be bred to create new assets or sell it for Ether.

Follow these steps:

1. In your, Brave web browser, go to www.cryptokitties.co.

2. Click Start.

3. Click Connect.

4. Click Sign In.

5. Click Sing in the popup window.

Purchasing CryptoKitties

In this section, you find two kitties to purchase. This will allow you to "breed" a new kitty and lease out your cats to others to breed.

Follow these steps:

1. In your, Brave web browser, go to www.cryptokitties.co.

2. Click Sign In.

3. Click Sing in the popup window.

4. Under Great-Value Kitties, click Browse All.

TIP

5. **Select a cute cat.**

   You have a lot of options, but because this exercise is mostly just for fun, be cheap. Also, look for a kitty that is "Swift" and "low-gen." They're faster at breeding and have shorter cooldown times between breeding.

6. **Click Buy Now.**

7. **Click OK, Buy This Kitty.**

8. **Click Confirm.**

9. **Select your second cat and follow the buy instructions.**

Breeding your CryptoKitties

In this section, you'll take the two cats that you purchased in the preceding section and breed them to create a new kitty. This is a very interesting activity in that you're creating a new digital asset that is unique, has verifiable provenance, and can be traded on an open global market without an intermediary to facilitate the authentication or transfer.

Depending on the speed of the Ethereum network at the time you purchased your cats, it may take a few minutes to see them under Kitties. Be patient — they will show up. You can always check your transaction log to look at the status.

Follow these steps:

1. **In your, Brave web browser, go to** www.cryptokitties.co.

2. **Click Sign In.**

3. **Click My Profile.**

4. **Select one of your cats.**

5. **Click Breed.**

   Breeding is represented by an eggplant icon.

6. **Click Sire with My Kitties.**

7. **Click OK, Let's Get Started.**

8. **Click the box that says Select Your Kitty.**

9. **Select the other cat.**

10. **Click OK, Give Them Some Privacy.**

11. **Click Confirm in the popup window.**

Leasing your CryptoKitties

In this section, we'll be putting out one of your cats to breed in the market. By doing this, you're leasing your asset on an open market with no intermediaries. If one of your cats is still pregnant, select the other cat to be leased.

Follow these steps:

1. **In your Brave web browser, go to** www.cryptokitties.co.
2. **Click Sign In.**
3. **Click My Profile.**
4. **Select one of your cats.**
5. **Click Breed.**
6. **Click Sire to the Public.**
7. **Adjust the prices and time as desired or leave the default settings.**
8. **Click Done.**
9. **Click Confirm in the popup window.**

Congratulations! You've bought your first Bitcoin and traded it for Ether. You then purchased blockchain assets and created your own. Finally, you leased out your assets in an open global marketplace to earn more Ether. Except for your first purchase, all these actions were enabled on an open public blockchain and did not need a bank or intermediary to facilitate. If you enjoyed CryptoKitties, and you'd like to learn how to create your own blockchain-based game, you can go through a simple online tutorial that teaches you how to do everything. You can find this tutorial at https://cryptozombies.io.

Building a Private Blockchain with Docker and Ethereum

Private blockchains hold the promises of both having the benefits of a private database and the security of blockchains. The idea is most appealing for two reasons:

>> **Private blockchains are great for developers because they allow them to test ideas without using cryptocurrency.** The developers' ideas can remain a secret as well, because the data has not been published publicly.

> » Large institutions can capitalize on the security and permanence of blockchain technology without their transactions being public the way they are in traditional blockchains.

TIP

Most of this book assumes you're just learning about blockchain for the first time and have little to no programing skills, but this section requires some knowledge of GitHub, Docker, and how to use your computer's terminal. If you need a quick recap on coding before you dive in, I recommend *Coding For Dummies* by Nikhil Abraham (Wiley) for a great overview on coding for nontechnical people. If you don't plan to ever be hands-on with blockchain technology, you might want to skip the rest of this chapter.

In this section, you dive into building your first blockchain. You build it in two steps. The first step is to prepare your computer to create your private blockchain. Don't worry — it's made easier with tools from Docker and work that has been done by talented developers on GitHub. The second step is building your blockchain inside your Docker terminal.

Preparing your computer

You need to download some software on to your computer in order to try this blockchain project. Start by downloading the Docker Toolbox. Go to `www.docker.com/toolbox` to download the correct version for your operating system.

Next, download GitHub Desktop. Go to `http://desktop.github.com`. After you've installed GitHub Desktop, create a GitHub account at `www.github.com` by clicking Sign Up and entering a username, email address, and password, and then clicking the Sign Up for GitHub button.

Now you need to create a place to store your blockchain data. Create a folder on your computer's desktop called `ethereum`. You'll use this folder to hold your future repository and other files. Follow these steps to complete the process:

1. **Open GitHub Desktop.**

2. **Sign into the GitHub Desktop application on your computer with your new GitHub account.**

3. **Return to your web browser and go to** `www.github.com/Capgemini-AIE/ethereum-docker`.

   You see the page shown in Figure 3-1.

4. **Click the Clone or Download button.**

   You'll be given two choices: Open in Desktop or Download Zip (see Figure 3-2).

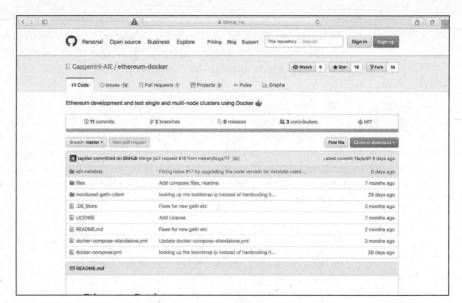

FIGURE 3-1:
Navigate to this
page at GitHub.

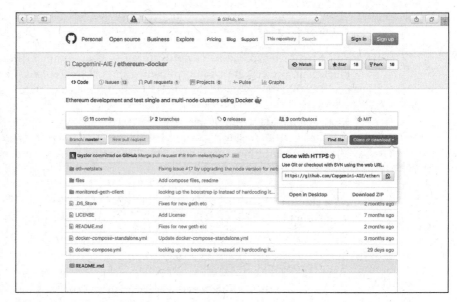

FIGURE 3-2:
Open in Desktop.

5. **Select the Open in Desktop option.**

   The GitHub Desktop application will reopens.

   In the GitHub Desktop application, navigate to the project folder
   ethereum **and click Clone.**

Cloning from GitHub copies the information you need to build your new blockchain. Follow the steps in the next section to get started building your private blockchain.

Building your blockchain

You're going to use the free Docker Quick Start Terminal tool to build your blockchain. It gives you access to a virtual machine, cutting down the time required to set up and debug your system. Because of these features, it lets you create a stable environment for your blockchain, so you don't have to worry about the settings on your machine, and you can get up and running faster.

Follow these steps:

TIP

1. **Launch Docker on your computer using the Docker Quick Start Terminal.**

   The Quick Start Terminal should be located with your applications or on your desktop.

   The Docker application launches a terminal you will use to build your blockchain.

2. **Change directories in the terminal to** `ethereum`**.**

   The files you create making the new blockchain will go into the desktop file you made in the preceding section. You need to give a command to the terminal in order to change directories. If you're on a Mac or running Linux, enter the following command:

   ```
   cd ~ /Desktop/ethereum/ethereum-docker/
   ```

   If you're on a PC, enter the following command:

   ```
   cd ~ \Desktop\ethereum\ethereum-docker\
   ```

TIP

   If these commands don't work for some reason, search the web for tutorials that explain how to change directories for your type of system.

   Now you can utilize the Ethereum-Docker files.

3. **Create one standalone Ethereum node by entering the following command into your terminal:**

   ```
   docker-compose -f docker-compose-standalone.yml up -d
   ```

This one line of code will have created the following:

- One Ethereum bootstrapped container

- One Ethereum container that connects to the bootstrapped container

- One Netstats container with a web UI to view activity in the cluster

4. **Take a look at your new blockchain by opening a web browser and going to** `http://$(docker-machine ip default):3000`.

Congratulations! You've built your own private blockchain. If you're so inclined, say a word of thanks to Graham Taylor and Andrew Dong, who put a lot of time into creating the Ethereum–Docker integration.

2
Developing Your Knowledge

IN THIS PART . . .

Discover the beginning of blockchain technology with the Bitcoin blockchain.

Clarify your knowledge of the Ethereum network, and expand your understanding of decentralized autonomous organizations and smart contracts.

Identify the core concept of EOS and how it's building a new platform for creating blockchain applications that scale.

Evaluate the Factom blockchain and its ability to secure data and systems.

Explore the Waves blockchain platform and learn how to create your own tokens and trade them.

Chapter **4**

Beholding the Bitcoin Blockchain

Warning! After reading this chapter, you may become hooked on this cool emerging technology. Read at your own peril.

Bitcoin demonstrates the purest aspects of blockchain technology. It's the baseline that all other blockchains are compared to and the framework that nearly all have drawn upon. Knowing the basics of how the Bitcoin blockchain operates will allow you to better understand all the other technology you encounter in this ecosystem.

In this chapter, I fill you in on the fundamentals of how the Bitcoin blockchain operates. I offer safety tips that will make your Bitcoin experience smoother and more successful. I also show you practical things you can start doing now with Bitcoin. In these pages, you find out how to mine the Bitcoin token, giving you a new way to get your hands on Bitcoins without buying them. Finally, you discover how to transfer your tokens to paper wallets, and other practical ways to keep your tokens safe online.

Getting a Brief History
of the Bitcoin Blockchain

Bitcoin and the concept of its blockchain were first introduced in the fall of 2008 as a whitepaper and later released as open-source software in 2009. (You can read the Bitcoin whitepaper at `www.bitcoin.org/bitcoin.pdf`.)

The author who first introduced Bitcoin in that 2008 whitepaper is an anonymous programmer or cohort working under the name of Satoshi Nakamoto. Nakamoto collaborated with many other open-source developers on Bitcoin until 2010. This individual or group has since stopped its involvement in the project and transferred control to prominent Bitcoin core developers. There have been many claims and theories concerning the identity of Nakamoto, but none of them have been confirmed as of this writing.

Regardless, what Nakamoto created is an extraordinary peer-to-peer payment system that enables users to send Bitcoin, the value transfer token, directly and without an intermediary to hold the two parties accountable. The network itself acts as the intermediary by verifying the transactions and assuring that no one tries to cheat the system by spending Bitcoins twice.

Nakamoto's goal was to close the large hole in digital trust, and the concept of the blockchain was his answer. It solves the Byzantine general's problem, which is the ultimate human problem, especially online: How do you trust the information you are given and the people who are giving you that information, when self-interest, malicious third parties, and the like can deceive you? Many Bitcoin enthusiasts feel that blockchain technology is the missing piece that will allow societies to operate entirely online because it reframes trust by recording relevant information in a public space that cannot be removed and can always be referenced making deception more difficult.

Blockchains mix many old technologies that society has been using for thousands of years in new ways. For example, cryptography and payment are merged to create cryptocurrency. *Cryptography* is the art of secure communication under the eye of third parties. Payment through a token that represents values is also something humans have been doing for a very long time, but when merged, it creates cryptocurrencies and becomes something entirely new. Cryptocurrency lets you take the concept of money and move it online with the ability to trade value securely through a token.

Blockchains also incorporate *hashing* (transforming data of any size into short, fixed-length values). Hashing also incorporates another old technology called Merkle trees, which take many hashes and squeeze them down to one hash, while still being able to prove each piece of data that was individually hashed (see Figure 4-1).

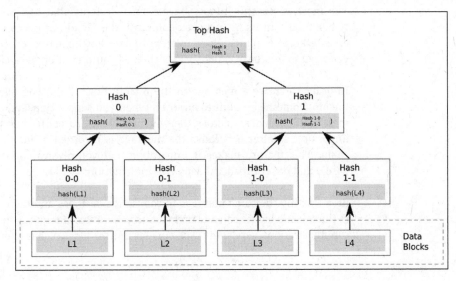

Ultimately, blockchains are ledgers, which society has been using for thousands of years to keep financial accounts. When all these old models are merged and facilitated online in a distributed database, they become revolutionary.

Bitcoin was designed primarily to send the Bitcoin cryptocurrency. But very quickly, the creators realized that it had a much larger potential. With that in mind, they architected the blockchain of Bitcoin to be able to record more than the data concerning the movement of the token. The Bitcoin blockchain is the oldest, and one of the largest, blockchains in the world. It's composed of thousands of nodes that are running the Bitcoin protocol. The protocol is creating and securing the blockchain.

REMEMBER

In very simple terms, the *blockchain* is a public ledger of all transactions in the Bitcoin network, and the *nodes* are computers that are recording entries into that ledger. The *Bitcoin protocol* is the rules that govern this system.

Nodes safeguard the network by mining for the cryptocurrency Bitcoin. New Bitcoins are created as a reward for processing transactions and recording them inside the blockchain. Nodes also earn a small fee for confirming transactions.

Anyone can run the Bitcoin protocol and mine the token. It's an open-source project that thrives as more individuals participate in the network. The fewer people who participate, the more centralized it becomes — and centralization weakens the system. The primary thing that makes Bitcoin a secure system is the large number of independent nodes that are globally distributed.

The most successful miners have robust systems that can outperform slower miners. Early in its history, you could run the Bitcoin protocol and earn Bitcoins on a desktop computer. Now, in order to have any hope of ever receiving Bitcoins, you need to purchase expensive specialized equipment or use a cloud service.

In order to create a message in the Bitcoin blockchain, you have to send some Bitcoin from one account to another. When you send a transaction in Bitcoin, the message is broadcast across the whole network. After the message is sent, it's impossible to alter it because the message is recorded inside the Bitcoin blockchain. This feature makes it imperative that you always choose your message wisely and never broadcast sensitive information.

Broadcasting the same message to thousands of nodes and then saving it forever in the token's ledger can add up in a hurry. So, Bitcoin requires that you keep your communications very short. The current limit is just 40 characters.

The New Bitcoin: Bitcoin Cash

There is significant conflict around the core development of Bitcoin. Dubbed the "Bitcoin Civil War" or the "block size limit debate," the general conflict is between keeping Bitcoin core as it is and enlarging the functionality of the software. This conflict appears simple, but the repercussions are enormous. Bitcoin's permanent nature and the billions of dollars' worth of assets that Bitcoin software secures mean that every code change is rigorously reviewed and debated.

Bitcoin hard-forked and split into two separate blockchains in 2017. The community of developers and Bitcoin miners couldn't agree on how to address growth. Bitcoin had become increasingly unreliable and expensive to use. It had once been a nearly instant and almost free system; now transactions were costing more than $50 and taking hours to days to clear. The high cost and slow speed drove away users.

A primary issue was that Bitcoin's transaction speeds were too slow, at seven transactions per second, to meet the demand on the network. Transaction fees climbed as users competed to have their transactions processed faster. One of the limiting factors was that Bitcoin's block size limit was 1MB in 2017.

Bitcoin Cash used the same codebase as Bitcoin but adjusted the block size limit. They increased the block size to 32MB. At the time of the fork, anyone holding Bitcoin was also given the same number of Bitcoin Cash. The increase was controversial because it disenfranchised smaller miners who had slower equipment.

Many miners feared that they couldn't be competitive mining larger blocks. There was also concern that the larger block size would lead to centralization of the Bitcoin blockchain network.

Bitcoin is a living and ever-changing system. The Bitcoin core development community is actively seeking ways to improve the system by making it stronger and faster. Anyone can contribute to the Bitcoin protocol by engaging on its GitHub page (`www.github.com/bitcoin`). However, there is a small community of dominant core developers of Bitcoin. The most prolific contributors are Wladimir Van Der Laan, Pieter Wuille, and Gavin Andresen.

THE LIMITATIONS OF BITCOIN

Blocks that make up the Bitcoin blockchain are limited to 1MB in size. This limits the number of transactions that the Bitcoin blockchain can handle to seven transactions per second. New blocks occur on average about every ten minutes, but they aren't guaranteed.

These limitations are hard-coded into the Bitcoin protocol and help ensure that the network stays decentralized. And decentralization is key to Bitcoin's robustness. Larger blocks would impose hardships on the miners and might push out small operations.

Bitcoin has built-in limitations that prevent it from handling the global volume of monetary transactions. It is also being used to secure other types of data and systems. The demand to use the secure Bitcoin ledger is high. This difficulty is referred to as *Bitcoin bloat,* and it has slowed down the network and increased the cost of transactions.

At this point, most blockchain developers are only experimenting with expanding the utility of the Bitcoin blockchain. Most are not at a point where they need to scale up their prototypes and concepts so that the Bitcoin blockchain can handle their request. Other new blockchain technologies have also helped bring down the pressure on Bitcoin and given developers cheaper options to secure data.

Debunking Some Common Bitcoin Misconceptions

People are often suspicious of anything new, especially new things that aren't easy to understand. So, it's only natural that Bitcoin — a totally new currency unlike anything the world had ever seen before — would confound people, and a few misconceptions would result.

Here are some of the misconceptions you might have heard about Bitcoin:

>> **Bitcoin was hacked.** There was one known instance in 2011 where someone double spent their Bitcoin, but it was resolved within an hour. Since this issue, there have been no known successful attacks on the Bitcoin blockchain that resulted in stolen Bitcoins. However, many central systems that use Bitcoin have been hacked. And wallets and Bitcoin exchanges are often hacked due to inadequate security. The Bitcoin community has fought back by developing elegant solutions to keep their coins safe, including wallet encryption, multiple signatures, offline wallets, paper wallets, and hardware wallets, just to name a few.

>> **Bitcoin is used to extort people.** Because of the semi-anonymous nature of Bitcoin, it's used in ransomware attacks. Hackers breach networks and hold them hostage until payment is made to them. Hospitals and schools have been victims of these types of attacks. However, unlike cash, which was favored by thieves in the past, Bitcoin always leaves a trail in the blockchain that investigators can follow.

- **Bitcoin is a pyramid scheme.** Bitcoin is the opposite of a pyramid scheme from the point of view of Bitcoin miners. The Bitcoin protocol is designed like a cannibalistic arms race. Every additional miner prompts the protocol to increase the difficulty of mining. From a social point of view, Bitcoin is a pure market. The price of Bitcoins fluctuates based on market supply, demand, and perceived value. Bitcoin is not a pyramid scheme, but there are many scams surrounding Bitcoin so be careful.

- **Bitcoin will collapse after 21 million coins are mined.** Bitcoin has a limit to the number of tokens it will release. That number is hard-coded at 21 million. The estimated date of Bitcoin issuing its last coin is believed to be in the year 2140. No one can predict what will happen at that point, but miners will always earn some profit from transaction fees. Plus, users of the blockchain and the Bitcoins themselves will be incentivized to protect the network, because if mining stops, Bitcoins become vulnerable and so does the data that has been locked into the blockchain.

- **Enough computing power could take over the Bitcoin network.** This is true, but it would be extremely difficult, with little to no reward. The more nodes that enter the Bitcoin network, the harder this type of attack becomes. In order to pull this off, an attacker would need the equivalent of all the energy production of Ireland. The payoff of this sort of attack is also extremely limited. It would only allow the attacker to roll back his own transaction. He couldn't take anybody else's Bitcoins or fake transactions or coins.

- **Bitcoin is a good investment.** Bitcoin is a new and interesting evolution in how people trade value. It isn't backed by any single government or organization, and it's only worth something because people are willing to trade it for goods and services. People's willingness and ability to utilize Bitcoin fluctuates a lot. It's an unstable investment that should be approached cautiously.

Bitcoin: The New Wild West

The Bitcoin world is much like the early days of the Wild West. It's best to approach cautiously until you figure out who the good guys and bad guys are and which saloon serves the coldest beer. If you fall victim to a scam, you'll have little to no protection.

WARNING

Bitcoins and other decentralized cryptocurrencies are considered currency in many countries, but there is little to no oversight or protection in place for consumers.

In this section, I list three of the common scams that are prevalent in the crypto-currency world. They all revolve around stealing your coins and look a lot like traditional cons you might already be familiar with. This list isn't exhaustive, and crooks are nothing if not creative, so be very cautious when using Bitcoins. You never know what's around the next corner.

Fake sites

Websites that look like exchanges or web wallets but are fakes have plagued some of the top Bitcoin websites. This type of scam is common in the Bitcoin world and on the web in general. Scammers hope to make money by stealing login informa-tion from users or misleading them into sending Bitcoins.

TIP

Always double-check the URL and only use secure websites (those that start with `https://`) to avoid this problem. If a website or claim seems doubtful, check to see if it's listed on Badbitcoin.org (`www.badbitcoin.org`). This is not an exhaustive list, but has many of the bad players listed.

No, you first!

"Send me your Bitcoins, and then I'll ship you the goods." Smells fishy, right? Scams like this are similar to money wire fraud. In this type of fraud, an individual pretends to sell you something but never delivers.

The semi-anonymous nature of Bitcoins — combined with the inability to do a charge back — make it tough to get your money back. Plus, governments do not currently offer protection for Bitcoin transactions, so you're up that proverbial creek without a paddle.

Fraudsters will try to win your trust by sending fake IDs or even impersonating other people you may know. Always double-check the information they send you.

TIP

The best way to dodge this sort of scam is to listen to your instinct and never put more Bitcoins at risk than you're willing to lose. If there is a way to verify the identity of the person offline, do so.

Get-rich-quick schemes

Crazy get-rich-quick schemes have proliferated the cryptocurrency world. The good news is: It's easy to recognize them if you know what to look for.

Often, you'll be promised massive returns, and there is some kind of recruitment and indoctrination process. This process could include things like sales training, asking you to recruit your friends and family, and promising that this is a risk-free investment and that you'll never lose your money. This includes never give anyone access to your private keys.

The bottom line: If a scheme looks too good to be true, it probably is. No matter what, take a hard look at how the investment is generating value outside of what you'll receive from your investment. If there is no clear and rational reason that a significant amount of value is generation rate, it's a scam.

TIP

Run all investments by a lawyer and a CPA. They can help you understand your risks and tax implications.

Mining for Bitcoins

You can get started earning Bitcoins in a variety of ways. Mining for Bitcoin is how to earn Bitcoins by participating in the network. It's usually handled by special mining hardware that is expensive and specialized. The equipment also needs Bitcoin mining software to connect to the blockchain and your *mining pool* (a collaboration of many miners jointly work together and then splitting the rewards of their efforts).

Here are three standard ways to explore mining Bitcoin:

>> **Bitcoin-QT:** The Bitcoin-QT client is the original software written by Satoshi Nakamoto. You can download it at https://bitcoin.org/en/download.

>> **CGminer:** CGminer is one of the most popular mining software. It is open source and available for Windows, Linux, and OS at www.github.com/ckolivas/cgminer.

>> **Multiminerapp:** The Multiminerapp is an easy Bitcoin client to run. You can download it at www.multiminerapp.com.

REMEMBER

Bitcoin is a very competitive environment, and unless you buy specialized mining equipment, you may never earn any Bitcoins. I don't endorse or recommend any particular mining equipment in this book because the industry is constantly changing and quickly out of date. Expect to pay between $500 and $5,000 per machine on average. Amazon.com is a good place to look. They have a large offering and many customer reviews to help guide you.

Cloud mining allows you to start earning bitcoins in an industrious afternoon, without the need to download software or buy equipment. Just follow these steps:

1. **Go to** https://hashflare.io/panel.

    The return on investment for cloud mining can be negative. Review your option carefully to make sure it is a positive investment.

WARNING

2. **Scroll down the home page and click the Buy Now button under SHA-256 Cloud Mining.**

    When I wrote this book, this option had the highest return on investment and the lowest startup cost. Take the time to reassess this on your own because this might have changed.

TIP

3. **Go through the sign-up process.**

4. **Link your bitcoin address.**

    If you haven't established a bitcoin address, turn to Chapter 3 and follow the directions to create a bitcoin wallet. You'll need to do this in order to claim your mining rewards.

5. **Buy a small amount of mining power.**

    This will allow you to join the bitcoin network.

6. **Join a mining pool.**

    This step allows you to get a faster mining reward than mining on your own. It pools the resources of several miners and then shares the prize between the pool.

Congratulations! Now just sit back and wait for your mining rewards to start rolling (or dripping) in.

Making Your First Paper Wallet

A *paper wallet* is a paper copy of your public and private key for your Bitcoins. Because they're completely offline, paper wallets are one of the most secure ways to hold Bitcoins when done correctly. The advantage is that your private key is not stored digitally, so it isn't subject to hacking. Making a paper wallet is fairly easy. Just follow these steps:

1. **Go to** www.bitaddress.org.

2. **Move your mouse around the screen until the amount of randomness shows 100%.**

3. Click the Paper Wallet button.

This gives the option to create a paper wallet that you can print.

4. In the Addresses to Generate field, enter 1.

You can make several wallets at once, if you need to, but you might as well just start with one to get the hang of it.

5. Click the Generate button.

Figure 4-2 shows a paper wallet I created.

6. Click the Print button.

WARNING

Do not let anyone watch you create your paper wallet. This isn't something you want to do at a public computer. Make sure to use a printer that is private and not connected to the Internet so you're not at risk of your private keys being hacked.

FIGURE 4-2:
A paper wallet.

TIP

Laminate your paper wallet to make it a little more durable.

Chapter **5**

Encountering the Ethereum Blockchain

The Ethereum project is one of the most developed and accessible blockchains in the ecosystem. It is also an industry leader in blockchain innovation and use cases. Understanding this technology is essential because it's leading the charge in smart contracts, decentralized organizations, and token offerings.

In this chapter, I cover the makeup of Ethereum and explain the new way to build organizations and companies on the Ethereum blockchain. I also go into depth on safety and practical business applications of the Ethereum blockchain. I fill you in on how the project started and where it plans to go.

This chapter sets you up to create your own decentralized organization. I explain how to mine the cryptocurrency on the test net to fuel your projects. After reading this chapter, you'll be able to set up your own Ethereum wallet and trade the token. You'll also be able to generate your own custom token that can be traded globally.

Exploring the Brief History of Ethereum

Ethereum was first described in 2013 in a whitepaper written by Vitalik Buterin, who was very active in the Bitcoin community as a writer and programmer. Buterin saw that there was significantly more potential in Bitcoin than the ability to move value without a central authority. He had been contributing to the colored coin effort within Bitcoin to expand the utility of Bitcoin beyond the trade of its native token. Buterin believed that other business and government use cases that require a central authority to control them could also be built with blockchain structures.

At that time, there was a fierce debate about the Bitcoin network being "bloated" by lots of low-value transactions from applications securing themselves against Bitcoin. The main concerns were that additional applications, built on the Bitcoin protocol, would have problems scaling in volume. Also, at that time there was not the ability to do scripting to allow for things like Smart Contracts. Bitcoin was not built to handle the number of transactions needed by the applications. Vitalik and many others saw that in order for people to build decentralized applications in the Bitcoin blockchain, either the blockchain would need a massive code overhaul or they would need to build a new blockchain altogether.

Bitcoin had already been well established at that point. It was clear that the kinds of upgrades to core code that were needed were well beyond what was realistically possible. The politics of Bitcoin would stall any changes to the network. Vitalik and his team established the Ethereum foundation in early 2014 to raise funds to build a blockchain network with a programming language built within it. Vitalik hoped to create a network that would allow him to build blockchain-secured applications.

The initial development was funded by an online public crowd sale during July and August of 2014. The foundation initially raised a record $18 million through the sale of its cryptocurrency token called *ether*. People have passionately debated whether this sort of crowd sale is illegal because it may constitute an unlicensed security offering.

The regulatory gray zone has not hindered the project. If anything, the cutting-edge nature of the project has attracted more attention and talent to the foundation. Discontented and disenfranchised developers and entrepreneurs from around the world have flocked to the project. Decentralization is seen as the perfect solution to corrupt and oppressive central authorities.

The $18 million raised in the token sale gave the foundation the funds it needed to hire a large development team to build Ethereum. Ethereum Frontier, the first release of the Ethereum network, went live to the public in July 2015. It was a bare-bones software release that only the more technically savvy could use to build their applications.

Homestead, the current Ethereum software release, was made available in 2016. It's much more user-friendly. Almost anyone can utilize the application template available on it. It has intuitive and user-friendly interfaces and a large, devoted development community.

Metropolis is the next planned Ethereum release. The main difference will be that applications will be fully developed and well tested. It will also feature even easier-to-use applications and have a larger market appeal where even nontechnical people will feel comfortable using it.

Serenity is the last planned phase of Ethereum development. It's where Ethereum will move from a *proof-of-work consensus* (in which miners compete to create the next block) to a *proof-of-stake model,* in which nodes are chosen pseudo-randomly with the possibility of being selected increasing based on their stake in the network. Their stake is measured by the amount of cryptocurrency in their possession. The main benefit of the change will be the reduction in the cost of energy associated with proof of work. This may make it more attractive for individuals to run nodes in the network, which would increase decentralization and increase security.

Ethereum: The Open-Source World Wide Computer

Ethereum may be one of the most complex blockchains ever built. It has several of its own *Turing-complete programming languages* (full-functioning programing languages that allow developers to create any application). These new programming languages closely resemble popular programming languages such as JavaScript and Python. The Ethereum protocol can do just about anything that your regular programming languages can do. The exception is that the code is written to the Ethereum blockchain and has the added benefits and security that comes with that. If you can imagine a software project, it can be built on Ethereum.

The Ethereum ecosystem is currently the best place to build decentralized applications. It has lovely documentation and user-friendly interfaces that get you up and running quickly. Rapid development time, security for small applications, and the ability for applications to easily interact with one another are key characteristics of this system.

The Turing-complete programming languages are the main feature that makes the Ethereum blockchain vastly more potent than the Bitcoin blockchain for building new programs. Ethereum's scripting language makes things like Twitter applications possible in few lines of code, and extremely secure.

Smart contracts, like the one you create in Chapter 3, can also be built on Ethereum. The Ethereum protocol has opened up a whole new genre of applications. You can take just about any business, government, or organization's processes and build a digital representation of it inside of Ethereum. Currently, Ethereum's platform is being used to manage *digital assets* (a new class of asset that lives online and may represent a whole digital asset such as a Bitcoin token or a digital representation of a real-world asset such as corn commodities), financial instruments (like mortgage-backed securities), recording ownership of assets such as land, and decentralized autonomous organizations (DAOs). Ethereum has also sparked a major fundraising effort by startups globally that used the ERC token standard to raise capital to build their innovations. Ethereum has opened a new way of organizing business, nonprofit, and government. It has made it possible to hold, share, and trade value without ever meeting the other party or using a third party to facilitate. The code does the work.

Decentralized applications: Welcome to the future

The most revolutionary and controversial manifestation of Ethereum is the self-governing and decentralized application (DAPP). DAPPs can manage things like digital assets and DAOs.

DAPPs were created to replace centralized management of assets and organizations. This structure has a lot of appeal because many people believe that absolute power corrupts absolutely. For those who are fearful of losing control, this type of structure has massive implications.

New DAPPs are popping up every day. You can explore and discover new ones built on Ethereum by going to https://dappradar.com. DappRadar updates a list of all the latest Ethereum Dapps and gives you a preview of what they do. One of the first ever created was Etheria (see Figure 5-1).

FIGURE 5-1:
The world's first immortal digital game, Etheria.

The power of decentralized autonomous organizations

DAOs are a type of Ethereum application that represents a virtual entity within Ethereum. When you create a DAO, you can invite others to participate in the governance of the organization. The participants can remain anonymous and never meet, which could trigger Know Your Customer (KYC) rules (the process a business must go through to verifying the identity of its clients) and anti-money laundering (AML; the laws and regulations designed to stop the practice of generating income through illegal means) compliance issues.

DAOs have been created for raising funds for investing, but they could also be designed for civic or nonprofit purposes. Ethereum gives you a basic framework for governance. It's up to the organizers to determine what's being governed. Ethereum has created templates for you to help in the creation of DAOs.

Figure 5-2 shows a depiction of the organization of an Ethereum application.

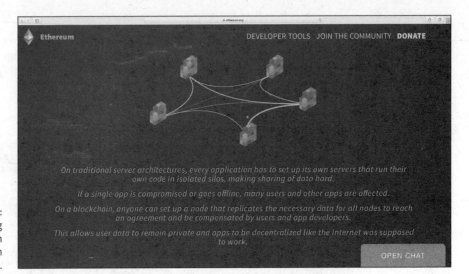

FIGURE 5-2:
Ethereum.org
blockchain
application
depiction.

On traditional server architectures, every application has to set up its own servers that run their own code in isolated silos, making sharing of data hard.

If a single app is compromised or goes offline, many users and other apps are affected.

On a blockchain, anyone can set up a node that replicates the necessary data for all nodes to reach an agreement and be compensated by users and app developers.

This allows user data to remain private and apps to be decentralized like the Internet was supposed to work.

OPEN CHAT

Here's how DAOs basically work:

1. A group of people writes a smart contract to govern the organization.

2. People add funds to the DAO and are given tokens that represent ownership.

   This structure works kind of like stock in a company, but the members have control of the funds from day one.

3. When the funds have been raised, the DAO begins to operate by having members propose how to spend the money. Voting may be affected by how much Ether the member risks or stakes in the DOA.

4. The members vote on these proposals.

5. When the predetermined time has passed and the predetermined number of votes has accrued, the proposal passes or fails.

6. Individuals act as contractors to service the DAO.

Unlike most traditional investment vehicles, where a central party makes decisions about investments, the members of a DAO control 100 percent of the assets. They vote on new investments and other decisions. This type of structure threatens to displace traditional financial managers.

DAOs are built with code that can't be changed on the fly. The appeal of this is that malicious hackers can't monkey with the funds in a traditional sense. Hackers can still find ways to execute the code in unexpected ways and withdraw funds. The immutable nature of a DAO's code makes it nearly impossible to fix any bugs once the DAO is live in Ethereum.

WITH GREAT POWER COMES . . . GREAT POWER

The first Ethereum DAO ever built is called, confusingly enough, "The DAO." It's an example of some of the dangers that come with decentralized and autonomous entities. It is the largest crowdfunded project in the world — its founders raised approximately $162 million in 26 days with more than 11,000 members. What people had thought was the greatest strength of The DAO became its greatest weakness. The immutable code within The DAO locked into place how the organization would be governed and how funds would be distributed. This allowed the members to feel secure in their investment. Although the code was well reviewed, not all the bugs had been worked out.

The first significant threat to Ethereum came from the hack of The DAO. An unexpected code path in The DAO's contract allowed any sophisticated user to withdraw funds. An unknown user managed to remove about $50 million before he could be stopped.

The Ethereum community debated bitterly about whether it could or should reclaim the ether. The DAO hacker had not technically done anything wrong or even hacked the system. Fundamentalists within the Ethereum community felt that code was law and, therefore, nothing should be done to recover the funds.

The very thing that made Ethereum strong was also its greatest weakness. Decentralization, immutability, and autonomy meant no central authority could decide what to do quickly. There was also no one to punish for the misuse of the system. It really did not have any consumer protection measures. It was a new frontier, like the software name suggested.

After spending several weeks discussing the problem, the Ethereum community decided to shut down The DAO and create a new Ethereum. This process is called *hard forking*. When the Ethereum community hard-forked the network, it reversed the transaction the hacker had committed. It also created a two Ethereums: Ethereum and Ethereum Classic.

Not everyone was in agreement with this decision. The community continues to use Ethereum Classic. The tokens for Ethereum Classic are still traded but have lost significant market value. The new Ethereum token still hasn't regained its old high from before the hack.

The decision to fork rocked the blockchain world. It was the first time a majority blockchain project had hard-forked to make whole an investor. It called into question many of the principles that make blockchain technology so attractive in the first place.

Hacking a Blockchain

Ethereum has never been hacked. The hard fork in 2016 due to the DAO hack mentioned in the "With great power comes . . . great power" sidebar was not an actual hack of the system, but confusingly is often referred to as a hack. Ethereum worked perfectly. The problem was it was too perfect. It became necessary to restart the system when a large amount of money and a majority of its users were threatened.

The only way to correct an action on a blockchain like Ethereum is to do a *hard fork*, which allows for a fundamental change to the protocol. A hard fork makes previously valid blocks and transactions invalid. Ethereum did this to protect the funds that were being pulled out of the first DAO by a user. The DAO hack was conceptually, one of the largest bug bounties ever.

That said, many scams and hacking attempts occur in the cryptocurrency space. Most of these attacks target centralized exchanges and applications. Many hackers want to steal cryptocurrency. It has real value and isn't protected in the same ways that regular money is protected by governments. The anonymous nature of cryptocurrency also makes it appealing to crooks. Catching and prosecuting these individuals is difficult. The cryptocurrency community is fight back, however, and creating new measures to protect themselves.

REMEMBER

Hacking one place is significantly easier and cheaper than trying to overcome a decentralized network. When you read about hacking in the blockchain world, it's likely just a website or a cryptocurrency wallet that has been hacked, not the whole network.

Understanding smart contracts

Ethereum smart contracts are like contractual agreements, except there is no central party to enforce the contract. The Ethereum protocol "enforces" smart contracts by attaching economic pressure. They can also enforce implementation of a requirement if it lives within Ethereum, because Ethereum can prove certain conditions were or were not met. If it doesn't live within Ethereum, it's much harder to enforce.

WARNING

Ethereum smart contracts are not yet legally enforceable and may never be because the perception is that you don't need outside authorities enforcing agreements. Legal systems are controlled by governments. As they stand now, governments are central authorities — some with more or less consent and democratic principles. Within an Ethereum smart contract, each participant has an inalienable vote.

Ethereum smart contracts do not include artificial intelligence. This is a cool possibility in the near future. But for now, Ethereum is just software code that runs on a blockchain.

Ethereum smart contracts are not safe. The DAO hack is a great example of the type of dangers that can occur. It is still early days, and putting a lot of money into an unproven system isn't smart. Instead, experiment with small amounts until all the bugs have been worked out of new contracts.

Discovering the cryptocurrency Ether

Ether is the name of the cryptocurrency for the Ethereum blockchain. It was named after the substance that was believed to permeate all space and make the universe possible. In that sense, Ether is the substance that makes Ethereum possible. Ether incentivizes the network to secure itself through proof-of-work mining, like how the token Bitcoin incentivizes the Bitcoin network. Ether is needed to execute any code within the Ethereum network. When utilized to execute a contract in Ethereum, Ether is referred to as *gas*.

Executing the code within a smart contract also costs some amount of ether. This feature gives the token added utility. As long as individuals want to use Ethereum for applications and contracts, ether will hold a value beyond speculation.

The wild growth in the value of ether has made it a popular token to speculate on. It's widely traded on exchanges around the world. Some new hedge funds are looking at it as an investment vehicle. However, the volatile nature and low market depth make ether a risky investment.

Getting Up and Running on Ethereum

In this section, I walk you through how to get started in the Ethereum blockchain ecosystem. Before you can build anything on Ethereum, you need an Ethereum wallet.

REMEMBER

Your wallet will hold your Ethereum tokens call *ether.* Ether is the cryptocurrency that allows you to create smart contracts inside Ethereum. This is sometimes referred to as *gas.*

Downloading the Ethereum wallet can take some time, but the interface is very intuitive and the instructions provided throughout the process are easy to follow.

TIP

Within the Ethereum wallet, you can win test ether to build your test contracts and organizations. You don't need to mine ether to learn how it works.

Mining for ether

Ethereum is kept running by a network of computers all over the world that are processing the contracts and securing the network. These computers are sometimes referred to as *nodes*, and they're mining crypto Ether.

In order to reward individuals for the time and cost involved in mining, there is a prize of five ethers about every 12 seconds. The prize is given to the node that was able to create the latest block in the Ethereum blockchain.

All new blocks have a list of the latest transactions. The proof-of-work consensus algorithm guarantees that prizes are won most often by nodes with the most computational power. Computers that aren't as powerful can win, too — it just takes longer. If you want to try your hand at mining ether, you can do it with your home computer, but it will take a very long time to successfully mine a block and win ether.

WARNING

Mining ether is not for the technical novice. You need to be familiar with command line. If you don't have a clue what command line is, you probably want to skip this process. Also, be sure to follow the most up-to-date instructions on the Ethereum GitHub (http://github.com/ethereum).

Setting up your Ethereum wallet

To set up your Ethereum wallet, follow these steps:

1. **Go to** www.ethereum.org.

2. **Click the Download button.**

   You have to scroll down the page a bit to find the button.

   Be sure to save the Ethereum wallet download someplace you can find it later.

TIP

3. **Open the Ethereum wallet.**

   You may need to check for updates to the software under Help.

4. **Choose Develop in the drop-down menu.**

5. **Select One of the Test Networks such as Robsten or Rinkeby.**

   Here you get set up to mine test ether. This process is much less time-consuming then real ether mining, but it still takes some time — currently, it's about two hours.

6. **Create a strong password.**

   Don't forget to save your password someplace safe.

7. **Click through the startup menu.**

   The Ethereum team has a few tutorials that are interesting to review while you're waiting on your test net to download. The download may take ten minutes or so.

8. **Choose Develop ⇨ Start Mining.**

   Don't skip this step. You need the ether for later projects.

You've just set up your wallet, and you're earning test ether for your future smart contract projects.

Building Your First Decentralized Autonomous Organization

DAOs will change how the world does business in the future. They allow anyone in the world to create a new type of company online that is governed by pre-agreed-upon rules that are then enforced through the blockchain network. Creating a DAO is easier than you might think. In this section, you build your first test DAO. I break this project into three sections: build, congress, and governance.

REMEMBER

In order to successfully complete your test DAO, you need to have set up your Ethereum wallet and done some mining on the Ethereum test net (see the preceding section).

Follow these steps to create your first test DAO:

1. **Go to** www.ethereum.org/dao.

2. **Scroll down the page to the Code box (shown in Figure 5-3) and copy the code.**

3. **Open the Ethereum wallet you made earlier.**

   You'll develop your DAO in your Ethereum wallet.

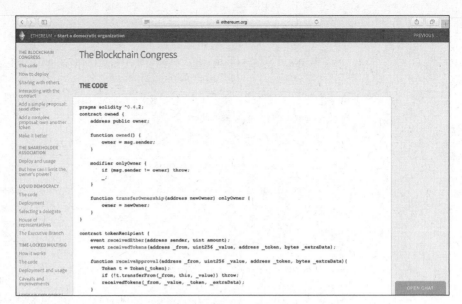

The Blockchain Congress

THE CODE

```
pragma solidity ^0.4.2;
contract owned {
    address public owner;

    function owned() {
        owner = msg.sender;
    }

    modifier onlyOwner {
        if (msg.sender != owner) throw;
        _;
    }

    function transferOwnership(address newOwner) onlyOwner {
        owner = newOwner;
    }
}

contract tokenRecipient {
    event receivedEther(address sender, uint amount);
    event receivedTokens(address _from, uint256 _value, address _token, bytes _extraData);

    function receiveApproval(address _from, uint256 _value, address _token, bytes _extraData){
        Token t = Token(_token);
        if (!t.transferFrom(_from, this, _value)) throw;
        receivedTokens(_from, _value, _token, _extraData);
    }
```

FIGURE 5-3:
The Code box.

Test net and congress

The next phase of your DAO project is setting up the framework for your DAO. Follow these steps:

1. **In your Ethereum wallet, choose Develop ⇨ Network ⇨ Test Net.**

2. **Click the Contracts tab and then click New Contract.**

   The Ethereum team has set up a few test templates for DAOs.

3. **Paste the code you copied in the preceding section into the Solidity code box.**

Make sure you're selecting Solidity Contract Source Code on the tab and not Contract Byte Code.

4. **From the Contract Picker, choose Congress.**

5. **Pick some variables when prompted to do so.**

   Here are your options:

   - The *minimum quorum* for proposals is the fewest votes a proposal needs to have before it can be executed.

   - The *minutes for debate* is the shortest amount of time, in minutes, that needs to pass before it can be executed.

   - The *margin of votes* for a majority. Proposals pass if there are more than 50 percent of the votes plus the margin. Leave it at 0 for a simple majority.

Governance and voting

Now you're going to name and set up the governance of your DAO. You need to set up a *minimum quorum* for proposals (how many votes a new proposal needs to have before it is passed). You also set up the *margin of votes for a majority* (how many votes a plan needs to pass) and the time allotted for discussing new plans.

1. **Name your new DAO.**

   This is kind of like naming a company.

2. **For Debate Times, select 5 minutes.**

   This is how long new proposals are open for conversation.

3. **Leave Margin of Votes for Majority set to 0.**

   This sets up how the democracy of your contract works.

4. **Confirm the price of the DAO.**

   You've mined some Ether in the test net via your wallet when you first set up it up. If you skipped that step, go back and do it now. You need a little of the test net Ether to build your DAO.

5. **Click Deploy and type your password.**

   The DAO may take some time to deploy. When you arrive at your new dashboard, scroll down, and you'll be able to see your DAO being produced.

6. **Click the New icon.**

   A new unique icon will generate that represents your DAO.

Congratulations! You've created your first DAO.

Uncovering the Future of DAOs

Smart contracts and decentralized organizations hold a lot of promise. The pure democratic and hyper-rational nature of them is very appealing. However, at this point, there are more possibilities then knowns, and each contract that is created could be groundbreaking or a massive flop.

If you approach Ethereum as the new frontier that it is, you'll have more success. The Ethereum network has more benefits than drawbacks if you're careful. But expecting everything to work flawlessly and all the participants to act with integrity will open you up to greater losses. Ethereum has its share of bandits, not to mention those friendly enthusiasts who would like you to succeed.

The smart contract hacks of 2016 have highlighted the importance of security and properly reviewing contracts. It also illustrated that there are people with integrity that who fight to fix issues.

Reading this book is only the beginning. It will give you a sound bases to build your knowledge of Ethereum, but as with all new technologies, Ethereum is quickly evolving. Keep reviewing best practices and security measures.

In the following sections, I mention some things to keep in mind as you build your first few DAOs, build smart contracts, and debug your new blockchain systems.

Putting money in a DAO

Don't trust large sums of money to untested and contracts and contracts that haven't been fully vetted. Large contracts are more often targeted by hackers. The DAO hack described earlier in this chapter (see the sidebar "With great power comes . . . great power") showed that even well thought-out contracts have unexpected weaknesses.

REMEMBER

Although, smart contracts and blockchains let you conduct business with anyone around the world, it's still the early days. You can mitigate your risk by working only with known and trusted parties.

TIP

The security landscape will constantly be evolving with new bugs. Reviewing all new best practices is imperative. Manage the amount of money you're putting at risk and roll out contracts slowly and in phases. Ethereum is a new technology, and mature solutions are not yet built.

Building smarter smart contracts

Smart contract programming requires a different mind-set than standard contract writing. There is no third party to make things right if the contract executes in a way that you didn't expect or intend. The immutable and distributed nature of blockchains makes it tough to change an unwanted outcome.

REMEMBER

Your contract will have flaws and may fail. Build safety valves into your contracts so you can respond to bugs and vulnerabilities as they come up. Smart contracts also need an off switch that let you pull the plug and pause your contract when things are going wrong.

TIP

If your contract is big enough, offer bug-hunting bounties that incentivizes the community to find vulnerabilities and flaws in your contract.

As with many things, the complexity of your contract also increases the likelihood of errors and attack vectors. Keep your contract logic simple. Build out small modules that hold each section of the contract. Creating a contract in this manner will help you compartmentalize any issues.

Finding bugs in the system

Don't reinvent the wheel by building your own tools such as random number generators. Instead, leverage the work that the community has already done and that has been well tested.

WARNING

You can only control for things within your own contract. Be cautious of external contract calls. They can execute malicious code and take away your control.

The Ethereum community has an excellent known bug list and even more helpful tips on how to build secure smart contracts on its GitHub page at https://github.com/ethereum/wiki/wiki/safety.

Creating Your Own ERC20 Tokens

In this section, I show you how to create your own token using Polymath. Polymath is a security token service that is built on the Ethereum blockchain. It has taken the hard work out of programming your own token on Ethereum. Polymath offers a point-and-click interface that anyone can use.

Before you read through this section, make sure that you've set up Meta Mask. If you haven't, refer back to Chapter 3, where you find detailed instructions for setting up your computer and downloading MetaMask.

You also need to get your hands on some Kovan Test Ether (KETH) in order to set up the smart contracts for your new token. KETH is the test Ether from the Kovan test network, a test network for developers working on Ethereum applications. KETH has no market value. You can obtain it for free if you have a GitHub account.

In this section, I walk you through how to set up your GitHub account, how to request KETH, and how to create your tokens.

Seeing up your GitHub account

GitHub is a development platform for storing code you develop. GitHub offers free accounts for open-source projects. So, if you're comfortable sharing the code you've developed, GitHub is a fantastic source for managing your projects and building software. GitHub also offers a paid version if you want to keep your code private. For the purposes of this section, a free account will work great.

To open a GitHub account, follow these steps:

1. **Open the Brave web browser.**

   If you don't yet have the Brave browser, go to Chapter 3.

2. **Navigate to** `https://github.com`.

3. **Enter your desired credentials.**

4. **Click Sign Up for GitHub.**

You're all set.

Requesting KETH on the Gitter Faucet

To request KETH, follow these steps:

1. **Open the Brave web browser.**

2. **Navigate to** `https://gitter.im/kovan-testnet/faucet`.

3. **Click Sign In to Start Talking.**

4. **Select Sign In with GitHub.**

Next, you'll grab your MetaMask account address so you can paste it into the social chat window and allow one of the community members to send you some KETH. Follow these steps:

1. **Open your MetaMask account.**

REMEMBER

   To open your MetaMask account, click the fox icon in the upper-right corner of your Brave browser window.

2. **From your MetaMask account, click the pull-down tab.**

3. **Select Kovan Test Network.**

4. **Copy your MetaMask address by clicking Account 1.**

Now you're ready to request some test Ether called KETH form the Kovan community. You'll take your Kovan Ethereum address from your MetaMask account and post it in the chat window. Make sure to only post your address. Follow these steps:

1. **Navigate back to** `https://gitter.im/kovan-testnet/faucet`.

2. **Paste your copied address into the chat window.**

Now you'll need to wait because one of the community members will check out your GitHub account and make sure you aren't spamming the network. This may take some time because the process of sending you KETH is done manually. You'll see the KETH in your MetaMask account after the transaction is complete. This process took me three days, but I worked on it over a holiday weekend.

To set up your Polymath account, follow these steps:

1. **Open the Brave web browser.**

2. **Navigate to** `https://tokenstudio.polymath.network`.

3. **Click Create Your Security Token.**

4. **Navigate to the fox icon for your MetaMask wallet.**

5. **Click Sign from within MetaMask.**

Creating your tokens

Now that you have the prerequisite KETH needed to create your own token, you can finally get started. In this section, you use the Polymath smart contract to build a custom Ethereum ERC20 token.

Reserving your token symbol

Polymath allows you to reserve your token symbol for 60 days. This reservation process is essential for setting up your token. You can check what names have already been taken by going to Etherscan (`https://etherscan.io/token`) and searching for the name you're thinking about using.

TIP

Reserving your name with Polymath only protects you within the Polymath system. It will not prevent someone else from issuing a token of the same name on Ethereum.

Go into your Jaxx wallet and use the Shapeshift service to exchange some of your BTC or Ether for POLY. After you've done this, move your new POLY tokens from your Jaxx wallet to your MetaMask account. (Chapter 3 gives instructions on how to move tokens from one address to another.)

To name your token, follow these steps:

1. **Enter your desired Token ticker name.**

   This needs to be five characters or less.

2. **Enter the name of your token.**

3. **Click Reserve Token Symbol.**

   This is a few letters that will represent your token on the network.

4. **Click Confirm.**

5. **Navigate to the fox icon for your MetaMask wallet.**

6. **Click Approve on Contract.**

7. **Click Approve on Fee.**

If your transaction will not approve, check to make sure you have enough Ether in your wallet to pay the Ethereum mining fee. It will take some time for your contract to be approved. This is because of the latency inherent in blockchains.

Creating your tokens

Now that you've reserved the name that you want to use for your token, you can create your new token. Polymath will have sent you an email with a link to your token creation dashboard.

WARNING

Your dashboard is integrated with several service providers that provide advisory, legal, KYC/AML, marketing, and custody service that you may need if you plan on making your token available to the public. KYC (Know Your Customer) is an anti-money laundering procedure used to identify customers that would like to move money. It's part of a global effort to fight money laundering and terrorism called AML (Anti-Money Laundering) and Combating Financing Terrorism (CFT). Always do your due diligence and seek your own legal counsel. If you choose to work with these integrated providers, the information you enter in each form will be sent automatically to the firms you selected. The firms will reach out to you to help you through the next steps.

In the following steps, I'm assuming that you are *not* going to offer your token to the public.

1. **Navigate to the Polymath email you received.**

2. **Click the link Click Here to Continue with your Token Creation.**

3. **Open your MetaMask wallet.**

4. **Click Sign.**

5. **Click I Have My Own for each of the service providers.**

Now that you've confirmed that you have your own service providers, you can start specifying your token. The left side of the page several icons that let you know where in the process you are.

1. **Click Token on the left side of the page.**

2. **Under My Security Token Must Be, click Divisible.**

3. **Click Create My Security Token.**

4. **Open your MetaMask wallet and click Confirm.**

5. **Click Confirm.**

6. **Wait a minute, and open your MetaMask wallet again and click Confirm for the mining fee.**

If the page is stuck on approving your contract for more than five minutes, refresh the page and use MetaMask to sign on again. Also, from inside your MetaMask wallet, you can see the status of your contract. You can increase the mining fee and have it processed faster. This can skyrocket the cost of the transaction, though, so be thoughtful if you choose this option.

Polymath has built-in distribution for tokens for those who are using them as a means of raising capital. On your Polymath dashboard, this is referred to as STO, shot for *Security Token Offering.* In the instructions I've provided, I made the assumption that the token you're creating will not be used for raising capital, so you can click Skip Minting and then click Confirm.

Polymath has created templates for the creation of security tokens. In these instructions, you use the smart contract that creates a hard cap of the number of tokens generated by the smart contract. You set a time and number of tokens that you would like to create. Because these tokens will be going to your own address, use minimum numbers so as not to waste your Ether.

Now you'll create a capped custom security token. The cap refers to the fact that the total number of tokens created is a fixed number that you choose at the time of its creation. Follow these steps to get started:

1. **Select the time current time.**

   Give yourself a few hours to input the transaction just in case something happens that stalls you.

2. **Under Raise In, select ETH.**

3. **Under Hard Cap, enter the number of tokens you would like.**

4. **Under Rate, enter** 1000.

TIP

   Think of this as the fee for generating your new tokens. You'll be "buying" them from the smart contract. If you enter 1000 under Rate, then the cost to produce your new tokens will be 1 ETH for 1,000 new tokens.

5. **Under ETH Address to Receive the Funds Raised during the STO, enter your MetaMask address.**

6. **Click Deploy and Schedule STO.**

7. **Click Confirm.**

8. **Navigate to your MetaMask wallet.**

9. **Click Confirm.**

Getting your hands on your tokens

You'll receive an email from Polymath letting you know that you have successfully set up your token. When you get this email, follow these steps:

1. **Navigate to** https://tokenstudio.polymath.network.

2. **Sign on via MetaMask.**

3. **Click Token on the right side.**

4. **Under Mint Your Token, download the sample CSV file.**

5. **Open the CSV file.**

6. **Remove the dummy data.**

7. **Input your own Kovan Test Network address in its place.**

8. **Save your new CSV file.**

Now that you've inputted your address to receive your token, you can upload it to the same page that you downloaded the sample from:

1. **Navigate back to** https://tokenstudio.polymath.network.

2. **Sign on via MetaMask.**

3. **Click Token on the right side.**

4. **Click Upload File.**

5. **Click Confirm.**

6. **Open MetaMask.**

7. **Click Confirm.**

Congratulations! You've created your own test security token. Ethereum is a powerful tool, and with tools like Polymath, it's easier and faster to create the blockchain applications you want.

Chapter **6**

Riding the Waves Blockchain

I n this chapter, I introduce you to the Waves blockchain, a relatively new block-chain with extraordinary capabilities. The Waves team has merged several technologies — such as multi-asset wallets, decentralized exchanges, and cryptocurrency creation tools — in an easy-to-use and friendly user interface.

The Waves blockchain is an exciting place for developers to build because it has smart contract functionality and uses a next-generation consensus algorithm, giving it some of the highest speeds for a public blockchain. But you don't need to know how to code to get something out of Waves.

If you're interested in creating your own digital assets or trading on decentralized exchanges, this chapter is an essential read. Here, you find out how to secure your web wallet, transfer Bitcoin, earn cryptocurrency through leasing out your assets, and create your very own cryptocurrency.

TIP

After you've read this chapter, to learn even more about the Waves platform, go to https://docs.wavesplatform.com/en/overview/how-to-use-this-guide. html.

Seeing How the Waves Blockchain Differs from Other Blockchains

Waves is a public blockchain platform based on the Nxt proof-of-state (PoS) protocol. It's fully decentralized, transparent, and auditable. Anyone can use the platform to launch, distribute, and trade *colored coins*, which are like the tokens issued on Ethereum via smart contracts. Colored coins are used to represent anything you might want to trade on a blockchain (for example, stocks, bonds, commodities, or real estate). With a few clicks and a simple download, you can start creating all kinds of new cool things.

WARNING

Just because you can easily create tokens and colored coins doesn't mean that it's legal to distribute them. Always check with your lawyer before creating something that may be used as a financial instrument.

Waves secures its network by leveraging the balances of existing accounts to "forge" blocks. Instead of having people use specialized equipment to "mine" new cryptocurrency, Waves rewards cryptocurrency holders for validating blocks. These so-called "forgers" are given transaction fees instead of a block reward. The PoS algorithm has been popularized because it's efficient enough to be run on small devices like the Raspberry Pi. Plus, PoS doesn't have the same scalability and security issues that PoW systems have.

GETTING A BRIEF HISTORY OF THE WAVES BLOCKCHAIN

The Waves platform was created by Sasha Ivanov in 2016. He wanted to create blockchain software that was easy and intuitive for the average person to use. This was a controversial stance within the blockchain space because most blockchain software was built for end users who were comfortable with using command line and their computer's terminal. There was often an attitude prevalent within development teams that "if they aren't smart enough, they shouldn't get involved."

But a lot of people believed in Sasha's dream, and he raised approximately 30,000 BTC, about $18 million at that time, to create the Waves platform. He has since gathered one of the largest communities and claims to have 300,000 active users in 25 countries. He also has a team of 100 developers who are dedicated to improving the platform.

TECHNICAL STUFF

Specifically, many PoW blockchains are vulnerable to a 51 percent attack where a majority of the mining power is being generated by a few individuals who can then corrupt the records written in the blockchain's history. However, PoS systems have their own issues: A few parties could aggregate a majority of the value on the network and take it over. Weighing cost reduction, speed, and security are essential as you're looking at different platforms to use for your business.

Waves also implements a decentralized peer-to-peer exchange, a voting system, a messaging/chat system, and a decentralized Domain Name System (DNS). Many blockchains have one or two of these features. Waves has *all* of them on a newer network model.

Unleashing the Full Power of Waves

The Waves wallet is more than just a place that you can keep your Waves cryptocurrency. It also supports several other cryptocurrencies, including Bitcoin and Ethereum. The Waves wallet also gives you access to a decentralized exchange (see "Using a decentralized exchange," later in this chapter).

The Waves wallet also allows you to generate your colored coins without needing to do any coding. Colored coins function much like the ERC20 tokens covered in Chapter 5. They're structured differently than ERC20, but they function the same. Colored coins can be set up for one-time use, like a digital coupon, or circulate like a currency.

The Waves wallet is very user-friendly and easy to learn. You'll find it to be one of the simplest, yet most powerful, blockchain applications available to the average person.

TIP

You can get a downloadable version of the Waves wallet, which holds your private keys on your device and is a more secure option. It also lets you work offline. Waves also has a fantastic web wallet, which is only available online. In this chapter, I show you how to use the web version because it's the most straightforward and easy version of the wallet and because it has access to the decentralized exchange.

In this section, I walk you through how to set up and back up your Waves wallet. As a side note, Waves has a minimum limit of 0.001 Bitcoin to open a Bitcoin wallet. That's about $10 at the time of this writing.

Setting up your Waves wallet

The Waves client is the wallet that allows you to hold your Waves cryptocurrency, trade cryptocurrency, and create new assets. Because of the unique PoS system that Wave uses to secure its network, you can also lease your Waves and be rewarded with transaction fees from the network — all within your Waves wallet.

Here's how to set up a recovery system for your Waves wallet, called a *SEED phrase*:

1. **Go to the Wave client website** at `https://client.wavesplatform.com/create`.

2. **Click Continue with Web.**

3. **Click What You Need to Know about Your SEED.**

4. **Click Protect Yourself.**

5. **Click I Understand.**

6. **Click Continue.**

Backing up your wallet

In this section, you take important steps to protect your digital assets and ensure you always have access to them.

WARNING

Blockchain software works differently from other Internet sites that allow you to create an account. Most online accounts have recovery features that allow you to gain access if you lose your password. This isn't the case with cryptocurrency. You have ultimate control of your account and the assets that you hold in your wallet — and if you lose access to your wallet, you lose everything in it, forever.

Start by grabbing a pen and a piece of paper. Then, to back up your wallet, follow these steps:

1. **Write down your account name.**

2. **Write down your password.**

3. **Type your password and account name into the appropriate fields.**

4. **Click Continue.**

TIP

Protect your piece of paper from being damaged by laminating it, if you can. Don't create a digital copy or take a photo of your password or seed phrase. Millions of dollars have been lost by crypto enthusiasts who have taken shortcuts when backing up their wallets, myself included.

After you've created your account, you'll want to back it up with what a SEED phrase. Follow these steps to back up your account:

1. **Get a second piece of paper.**

2. **Click I Understand.**

3. **Write down on paper in order your 15 words that form your account SEED.**

4. **Click Continue.**

5. **Reorder your 15 words.**

6. **Click Confirm.**

7. **Check the boxes and click Confirm and Begin.**

Congratulations! You've now set up and backed up your account on Waves. Make sure to keep your username, password, and backup phrase (the 15 words you wrote down) in a safe place.

TIP

Your backup phrase is also known as your seed phrase. It can be used to restore your account if you've lost your password. Because no one can reset your account password for you, make sure never to lose your pieces of paper, and keep the 15-word phrase in a different place from your username and password.

Uncovering Your Wallet's Features

Now that you've set up and secured your account, you're ready to explore some of the fantastic features of the Waves wallet. The Waves wallet lets the persons outside of the United States buy cryptocurrency with a credit card. But everyone is allowed to hold multiple cryptocurrencies, trade assets on its decentralized exchange, transfer assets to other users, and create unique colored coins (which can be one-time use, like a digital coupon, or have a perpetual life, like a currency).

TIP

In the following section, I show you how to transfer Bitcoin to your new Waves wallet. I recommend using at least $10 to start, because Waves has a minimum amount before it will initiate the wallet for you. Double-check the fine print before sending any Bitcoin — the limit may have changed by the time you're reading this book.

I also show you how to use a decentralized exchange to trade your Bitcoin for Waves cryptocurrency.

Transferring crypto assets

If you don't yet own any cryptocurrency, you'll need to get some to continue exploring the Waves platform. In Chapter 3, you can get detailed instructions on how to obtain your first Bitcoin.

After you've obtained some Bitcoin or Ether, you can use it to purchase Waves cryptocurrency. And later, you'll use your Waves to create your very own colored coin. Conveniently, you can trade your Bitcoin or Ether from within your Waves web wallet without having to use a cryptocurrency exchange.

Before proceeding through this section, note the following:

>> Purchasing and using cryptocurrency has many unknown regulatory and tax implications that are still being hotly debated. Buying and trading cryptocurrency may create a tax liability.

>> Web wallets are not a very secure way to hold your assets. Only hold what you need for these exercises in your account at any time. Ten dollars of Bitcoin or Ether will be sufficient.

If you haven't yet set up your wallet on the Waves platform, do so now. Also, if you have haven't yet purchased Bitcoin, review Chapter 3 and set up a Coinbase account. Then follow these steps:

1. **Open two browser windows.**

2. **In one window, go to** www.coinbase.com **and log in to your Coinbase account.**

3. **In the other window, go to** https://client.wavesplatform.com **and log in to your Waves account.**

4. **Copy your Bitcoin address for your Waves account.**

5. **In your Coinbase window, paste your Bitcoin address.**

6. **Send $10 of Bitcoin to Waves.**

Transferring the Bitcoin from your Coinbase account to your Waves account may take some time. Waves also has a minimum limit of .001 Bitcoin to open a Bitcoin wallet. That's about $10 at the time of this writing.

Using a decentralized exchange

Decentralized exchanges, often called DEXs, do not require you to trust the exchange with your money or cryptocurrency. You hold your own assets within your wallet until you decide to sell them and a buyer decides to purchase them.

When you want to sell cryptocurrency using a DEX, first you have to write an order to the decentralized order book for that exchange. After you've written your order, another user can then add a digitally signed counterorder and buy your cryptocurrency. The completed transaction is written to the DEX's blockchain, and the assets are transferred between you and the buyer.

In this section, I introduce you to the innovations that have occurred on the Waves DEX system. I also show you how to trade your own Bitcoin for Waves using the Wave's DEX. Make sure to complete this section if you want to create your very own colored coin later in this chapter. You'll need Waves tokens to do so.

CENTRALIZED VERSUS DECENTRALIZED EXCHANGES

Centralized exchanges are targets for hackers because they're central repositories of large sums of value. Always be careful when using centralized exchanges and think twice when leaving large amounts of value on them. The reason for this vigilance is that your funds might not be there next time you go to trade.

One of the most famous cases of theft on a centralized exchange was the Mt. Gox heist. The Bitcoin exchange collapsed in 2014 after hackers compromised the central system. The thieves made off with approximately 650,000 bitcoins that have never been recovered. The exchange's collapse left the cryptocurrency community in shock. Since then, dozens of new central exchanges have popped up and been targeted by thieves.

Pioneers in the blockchain space through grit, determination, and creativity have developed many new solutions, including the Waves decentralized exchange. DEXs are not without their own faults. Many DEXs have low liquidity, and traders need to be able to quickly buy and sale in the market without affecting the asset's price. Many DEXs have no interoperability and can't gain a significant market share on their own. Often, DEXs are designed so they're fully integrated into a blockchain; this increases security but makes them reliant on the block speed of that particular blockchain. Their slow speed and the high transaction costs that come with full integration also makes them unattractive to traders. Other issues that decentralized exchanges are vulnerable to are arbitrage by traders who look to profit on the slight differences in price across exchanges. This type of trading can wipe out user's funds on DEXs.

New hybrid approaches, such as the Waves DEX, look to combine the value of a central exchange, such as high-speed trading, automatic order matching, and low cost, with the benefits of a DEX that enable the owners of assets to remain in custody of their assets until they're traded.

Trading on the Waves decentralized exchange

The Waves DEX allows you to trade assets from the security of your wallet. Because the Waves wallet supports several different types of cryptocurrency, you can trade them all on the Waves DEX — not just the Waves cryptocurrency and Waves colored coins. Trading has many of its own challenges and must be done thoughtfully.

The Waves DEX has fixed one of the many issues that have kept DEX technology from being more widely used. It has created real-time trading by centralizing the order book matcher. The Waves DEX is a hybrid of both centralized and decentralized exchange technology. Its centralized matcher pairs incoming orders and executes your trades typically within milliseconds. This is an advantage over other DEXs that are fully integrated within a blockchain. Fully decentralized exchanges are dependent on the block speed of their blockchains and have much higher trading costs.

You signal your willingness to purchase or sell assets by creating, signing, and sending a limit order request to the Waves matcher. The orders on Waves are the same as on other exchanges. An order for a buy is a fixed number of a token at a price equal to or better than you've specified. When you create a new order, it's submitted to the DEX. You order is checked for accuracy and your signature is validated by your wallet's public key.

The orders on the Waves DEX are linked in pairs and checked by Waves nodes. Then the matcher creates an exchange transaction, signs them, and writes the trade history into the Waves blockchain. You don't have to execute a full order. The Wave's matcher can also match partial orders. The validating nodes don't charge these partial orders a full order fee. Your assets are only transferred after the trade has been publishing in the Waves blockchain. If the matcher fails for some reason, your trade will not take place. All unfilled orders are canceled automatically after 30 days.

Exchanging Bitcoin for Waves

To trade Bitcoin from your Waves Bitcoin wallet for Waves cryptocurrency using the Waves DEX, follow these steps:

1. **Go to** `https://client.wavesplatform.com` **and log in to your account.**

2. **Click the Exchange icon.**

3. **Click Waves/BTC.**

4. **Input the minimum Waves/BTC order.**

5. **Click Buy Waves.**

6. **Click the Wallet icon.**

7. **Wait for your trade to execute.**

It may take a bit before you receive your Waves. You're waiting for your order to be matched with a seller at the price you put out. You'll know that your trade executed because on the wallet page, you'll notice that your Bitcoin balance has changed and your Waves balance has increased.

Congratulations! You just used a DEX to trade Bitcoin for Waves.

REMEMBER

Don't leave much value in an online wallet. And keep in mind that there may be tax implications for your trades.

Creating and Leasing Out Your Own Cryptocurrency

On the Waves platform, the cryptocurrency is colored coins. Colored coins have many uses. Anything that can be quantified and represented digitally for trade could use a colored coin as the mechanism for transfer its ownership online.

TECHNICAL
STUFF

Colored coins and tokens have much the same utility, and the terms are often used synonymously, but they're technically structured very differently. I always refer to Waves as colored coins so as to not confuse them with tokens that are generated on other blockchains through smart contracts.

In this section, you create your own colored coin using the simple colored coin generator that is built inside your web wallet. With a few clicks, you'll have created a unique asset that can live on independent of you for the life of the Waves platform. You don't even need to know how to code, but you do need to own some cryptocurrency already.

You may be able to buy Waves cryptocurrency from within your web wallet. This functionality is not available in all countries. If you skipped earlier parts of this chapter, go back now to obtain your first Waves. You will need at least 1 to generate tokens. Once you have some Waves tokens, follow these steps:

1. **Click the dice icon.**

   You'll know you're on the right page because it will say "Token Generation" at the top.

2. **In the Name of Your Asset Field, input a name for your new colored coin.**

3. **Add a description.**

4. **Enter the total number you would like generated.**

5. **Leave the drop-down menu on Reissuable.**

   This means that your colored coins will stay in circulation after creation and transfer to a new person.

6. **In the Decimals field, enter** 8.

   This is the smallest amount that can be handled with your new colored coin. Most cryptocurrencies are eight decimals.

7. **Click Generate.**

8. **Click Confirm.**

9. **Click View Details.**

Congratulations! You've created your very own colored coins. You can view them by returning to the asset page where your Bitcoin and Waves are listed, and clicking the plus icon on the lower-right side of the page. This will bring up an option to pin your new coin to your asset home page.

Now that you've created your colored coins, you can lease out a portion of your Waves cryptocurrency and participate in the community that secures and maintains the Waves network. The best part is that you can earn new Waves by staking them. Just follow these steps:

1. **Click Leasing.**

2. **Click Start Lease.**

3. **Click List of Nodes.**

4. **Choose a leasing pool.**

   There will be several. Select one with active users and that makes regular payouts.

5. **Click the name of the pool.**

6. **Copy the leasing address at the top of the page.**

7. **Paste the leasing address into the Recipient field.**

8. **Enter the number of Waves you want to lease.**

   If you want to lease all your Waves, click Max.

9. **Click Start Lease.**

10. **Click Confirm.**

When you want your Waves back, you can cancel the lease by clicking the Detail icon and clicking Cancel Leasing.

Chapter **7**

Finding the Factom Blockchain

The Factom blockchain is a powerful tool that will help industry scale block-chain technology. It's different from other public blockchains and has unique properties that make it ideal for publishing data streams and secur-ing systems. The Factom blockchain also has a corporation behind it — Factom, Inc. — which spearheads its development and builds tools and products on top of the protocol.

Factom software is being built into systems that govern identity and security of both people and things. They're integrating and bridging other blockchains and blockchain technology as well. Linking blockchain networks improves the security by increasing redundancy and makes the other blockchains more interoperable.

This chapter explains how Factom works, fills you in on its unique properties, and provides easy-to-follow instructions that will help you get started using it. After reading this chapter, you'll understand many of the core concepts of Factom blockchain technology and know where it will add value to your blockchain projects.

This may be the time to mention that I am a co-founder of Factom. Although my aim is objectivity, my enthusiasm for Factom is hard to hide.

A Matter of Trust

Blockchains at their core are about allowing different entities to cooperate and collaborate without needing to trust each other's data security or business processes. Historically, trusted middlemen or industry consortiums have enabled this to happen, but those have high overhead costs and merely shift the trust to a different party. Blockchains shift the trust to a network of disimpassioned third parties and, ultimately, math.

Factom, Inc., is a company that builds blockchain software on top of the open-access Factom blockchain. Factom's recordkeeping software works at a high level by publishing encrypted data or a cryptographically unique fingerprint of that data to the Factom blockchain (shown in Figure 7-1). Additional measures are taken to secure the network by publishing a hash of the whole Factom blockchain every ten minutes in multiple other public blockchains. This extra publishing feature makes Factom different from most public blockchains.

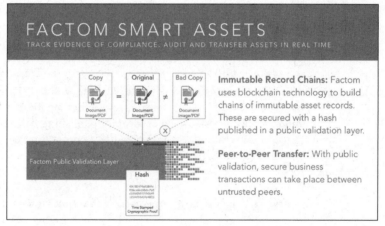

FIGURE 7-1:
The structure of the Factom blockchain.

Illustration courtesy of Factom, Inc.

The concept of the protocol was presented as a whitepaper in 2014 to address scalability issues of Bitcoin. As decentralized applications began securing themselves in Bitcoin, it became clear that entering data into the Bitcoin blockchain was prohibitively expensive at scale, and the Bitcoin couldn't handle high transactional volumes. There was no way to metaphorically get 10 pounds of data into the 5-pound Bitcoin bag.

The Factom protocol was designed to address the cost and volume limitations of other blockchains. The primary objective was to secure data and systems. Because of this objective, Factom is often described as a *publishing engine*. It allows users to write data to its ledger for a small fee. These entries are limited to 10 kibibytes and have a fixed cost that is less expensive and has more capacity for transaction volume by an order of magnitude compared to blockchains that use proof of work. The fixed cost of entering data into Factom is also a unique characteristic of Factom. Networks or other blockchain software that have one publicly traded token or cryptocurrency (as opposed to the two-token system that Factom utilizes) will have price differences dependent on the market cost of their token or cryptocurrency and how much demand there is on the network.

An important concept to understand is that the Factom blockchain is built in layers and chains. The layers have to do with how the data is structured. They use Merkle trees to leave cryptographic proof that any given data was published within Factom. The cryptographic proof, called a *Merkle root* (32 random characters that can represent a whole tree of individual data), is then published into other public blockchains like Ethereum. This is redundant security that other blockchains don't offer.

TECHNICAL STUFF

A Merkle tree is a mathematical tree constructed by hashing paired data and then pairing and hashing the results until a single hash remains, known as the Merkle root. This cryptographic proof was named after Ralph Merkle in 1979.

Organizing data into chains helps with scalability. Chains allow applications to only pull the data that they're interested in from the Factom blockchain, without needing to download the full data set. How they work is very simple: You can publish your data into an existing chain within Factom, or you can create a new chain. The chain ID is then used in the subsequent items you publish as a way to trace back the data you care about.

The purpose of the Factom blockchain: Publishing anything

Factom is a publishing platform. At its core, it was designed to publish and validate any data. All other tools on it are built around these simple functionalities. Factom can handle transactions that are up to 10 kibibytes; larger transactions need special structuring and require multiple entries. Alternatively, a hash that represents the data can also be published.

Because the Factom protocol is open source, the system acts as a public utility. It's a place where anyone can publish anything and be secured by the Factom blockchain. Not surprisingly, some individuals have published obscene content, but the limit on entry size means they can't publish much. And spam is curbed in the system by charging a small amount per entry. So if you want to swear in the blockchain, it'll cost you.

Factoids are the Factom network cryptocurrency. Decentralized systems need a reward mechanism to incentivize participants. Having this closed system requires cooperation, and builds the long-term network value creation. Factoids can be traded and purchased like any of the thousands of cryptocurrencies and tokens in the market. In the end, Factoids are used to purchase entry credits for the Factom Network.

The cost of an entry is fixed, while the cost of a *Factoid* fluctuates. As a Factoid increases in value, the user can buy more entry credits. This system allows users to be separated from tradable tokens and maintains fixed cost for consumers while allowing for a free market on the speculation of Factoids. This functionality was built into the initial release of Factom to allow heavily regulated industries and governments to utilize blockchain technology without dirtying their hands with tradable tokens.

As of early 2017, the Factom Network sees about 40,000 entries a day. These include things like the Russell 3000 Index and a record of altcoin prices each day. These records are used as historical references and can be utilized as input to smart contracts or to prove a historical timeline. These methods are being used in many places in the world. China has begun to reference Factom entries. And the U.S. Department of Homeland Security has also used Factom entries to help secure hardware.

Storing and accessing of data today is mostly a solved problem in the industry. Computer backups can be replicated and archived on a massive scale. A big problem that remains is determining which document is the most recent revision, especially across different organizations. With a blockchain-based document management system, organizations can ensure that they're using the same documents as their partners.

Incentives of federation

Many blockchains, such as Bitcoin and Ethereum, use a "proof-of-work" consensus. In this kind of blockchain, the consensus algorithm is how a blockchain comes to agreement on new data entered into the system. The consensus system examines whether new data is valid. Public blockchains need a robust system because anyone can add data to their blockchain. Blockchain consensus mechanisms are the rule set that determines what makes a valid block, entry and what chain should be trusted.

Proof-of-work (POW) has many characteristics that make it very attractive. It can often require a capital investment into specialized computer hardware and access to electricity (the cheaper, the better). This means that the only requirement to join as an authority in the system is to burn electricity with commodity hardware. It also means that in order to rewrite history, an equivalent amount of energy must be re-burned. This expense makes rewriting history unprofitable and, thus, unlikely.

Proof-of-work is excellent at securing blockchains. On the other hand, it consumes vast sums of energy and is expensive to operate. It's a cannibalistic arms race where the fastest computers win, and each additional gigahash added to the network increases the challenge.

The more data contained in each block, the more difficult it is to validate. Proof-of-work systems like Bitcoin also requires the full blockchain to validate a specific data point in the system. For others to prove the transaction you made in the Bitcoin blockchain is valid, they must have all of Bitcoin's blockchain downloaded. Currently, that takes several days.

Factom has a unique consensus system that steps back from the question, "Is an entry valid?" The Factom system instead uses elected consensus nodes that validate transactions by checking, "Has the entry been paid for?" The users of the system are the ones validating entries. Factom also structures data in subchains that can be parsed individually to prove the validity of any entry without downloading the full blockchain.

Figure 7-2 shows a diagram of the Factom chain structure.

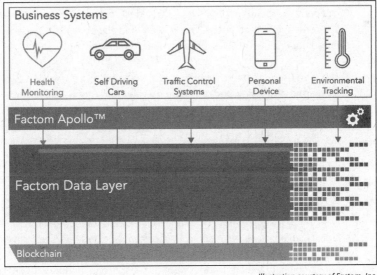

FIGURE 7-2:
The Factom chain structure.

Factom has been structured this way for commercial applications because members of one industry don't need to download all the irrelevant data about an unrelated industry. For example, verifying that all documents related to a mortgage have been accounted for does not also require downloading years of stock exchange history.

The Factom blockchain also spreads itself out to secure its network against data corruption. Every few minutes, it creates a small anchor into Bitcoin and Ethereum. This does two key things:

>> **First and most important, it prevents the servers building the Factom blockchain from undetectably rewriting history.** Because the servers can't control Bitcoin or Ethereum, any history they have recorded is permanent.

>> **It prevents the Factom servers from showing two different versions of the blockchain to different people.** Personal customization of web pages is something that Amazon and Facebook routinely do. Showing conflicting histories of business transactions to different companies is a recipe for misunderstanding. Because there is only one Bitcoin blockchain, that prevents altered versions of history from being created.

THE CRAZY EIGHT

Factom, Inc., began as a project to scale Bitcoin and moved into an enterprise software company that builds applications and products for government and large institutions. The company formed by the Factom team had eight original founders that came from a mixed background of sales, development, and engineering.

This is an unusually large founding team that needed a different way of governing, dividing responsibility, and distributing equity. They adopted *holacracy,* a management structure that closely resembles the decentralized networks that they built. Authority and decision-making are distributed among managers. The consensus is created weekly through a 45-minute management meeting.

The company is headquartered in Austin, Texas, and has global projects that involve identity, document management, real estate, and the Internet of Things (IoT). In each case, Factom is working on the record keeping and sharing. It has a partnership with Smartrac, a manufacturer and supplier of radio-frequency identification (RFID) products and IoT solutions, to secure *breeder documents* (documents, like birth certificates, that enable people to get other documents, like Social Security cards or driver's licenses) and prevent identity theft. It's working on IoT security and identity with the Department of Homeland Security and medical record management with the Gates Foundation.

Building on Factom

Factom was created for applications to be built on top of it. The primary purpose of many of the early blockchains was to secure their own data — that is, the history of the ownership of their cryptocurrency. Factom, on the other hand, was conserved first as a system that would allow blockchain software to scale. The primary issues that Factom addresses are speed and cost. Factom was also created to bridge other blockchains.

Authenticating documents and building identities using APIs

Factom has come out with a set of application programming interfaces (APIs) that can be used by development teams to manage and authenticate documents and build identities for people and things. You still need a developer to help you, and they're designed for enterprise integration, not ideal for a small project at this point.

You can use the APIs without needing to set up a blockchain or run a cryptocurrency wallet. It takes the headache out of the process and is ideal for those who are worried about the regulatory gray zone that cryptocurrency still falls under.

Getting to know the Factoid: Not a normal cryptocurrency

Factom has a unique two-token system, which uses Factoids and entry credits. The Factoid is a cryptocurrency that is traded on several markets just like Bitcoin. But it isn't a currency in the same sense as Bitcoin.

The Factoid's primary purpose is to be converted into entry credits. The network regulates the conversion of Factoids to entry credits at a fixed rate meant to keep cost down for users. Although Factom produces new Factoids in each block it creates, like other public blockchains, each entry made in Factom also removes Factoids from circulation. The Factom system effectively destroys Factoids. This process is called *burning*. When a Factoid is burned, it's removed from circulation.

Factoids fluctuate in price depending on speculation and utility. Entry credits, on the other hand, have a stable price that is maintained at US$0.001. This makes the fees paid to publish a predictable cost.

The Factom team issued some number of tokens during the crowd sale to raise funds for the core development of the protocol. The funds raised from the crowed sale were locked into an escrow that was overseen by a board of third-party reviewers that insured that the Factom team met its development goal before receiving the funds.

Anchoring your application

Blockchain technology has opened the doors for new products and services. The blockchains themselves serve as the base layer that old technology can reinvent itself with or innovation can be built on. Each blockchain has its own unique properties that make it ideal for specific applications.

Factom is particularly good at securing information, but it still has limitations: the size of each entry, and the fact that the more you publish, the more it costs. Factom is ideal for storing large files in a cloud solution and then using pointers within Factom to locate those files for your application.

Factom is primarily being used as a system to manage documents, data, and build identity. Each unique chain within Factom is a permanent history of that data (whatever that might represent) that has been entered to that specific chain. These "histories" are locked into an order that can't be manipulated. When an entry has been created and published, it can't be removed or manipulated. This is a powerful tool when you need to create chronological ordered histories. Because Factom is a public blockchain, anyone can make an entry against any chain. Software has been built that will look at each entry on a chain and disregard entries that have not been cryptographically signed — in effect, disregarding spam entries. Factom also integrates well with other blockchains, and it can be used to create an oracle for your smart contract that lets you reference other permanent data at a lower cost than that of proof-of-stake systems.

Publishing on Factom

Factom was built by developers for developers. It requires utilizing your terminal and downloading special software to both use your wallet and make entries into the network.

The team at Factom has been working hard to build a robust system first. They have documentation that will walk you through the process and a GitHub repository with all their open-source software for you to review and even contribute to. Efforts have been made to make Factom more individual consumer friendly, but that's still some time away.

TIP

FreeFactomizer is one of my favorite apps built by a Factom fan. It's very simple to use and allows you to check out the basic functionality of Factom without being a developer, opening a terminal, or doing any coding. It creates a hash of data that you enter into a text box or when you upload a file. It then gathers other hashes of documents submitted by other visitors. Every ten minutes, it combines all these hashes into an entry in the Factom blockchain. It offers a simple proof of existence.

REMEMBER

FreeFactomizer is a free service provided by an individual. It costs money to supply this service and may not be available in the future. There is also no warranty of any kind.

To use FreeFactomizer, follow these steps.

1. **Go to** www.freefactomizer.com.

    Figure 7-3 shows the FreeFactomizer home page.

2. **Upload a document to be hashed.**

    Use an unimportant document — one that doesn't contain sensitive information — because this service is not warranted or secure.

3. **Click Factomize the File Signature.**

    You're given a time estimate for how long it will take for the file to be added to Factom.

4. **Wait for the file to be added to Factom.**

    It take at least ten minutes for your file to be bundled with other documents and data. When this process is complete, FreeFactomizer will provide you a link back to Factom Explore.

5. **Check the entry by using Factom Explore, a search tool for the Factom database that allows you to look up entries.**

    Another option to try is to uploading the document again. It will send back a note like this: "->Signature already registered." This means that they have added it already to Factom.

Congratulations! You've just stored a fingerprint of data in Factom and explored its core functionality.

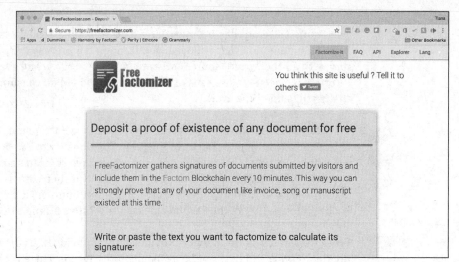

FIGURE 7-3: FreeFactomizer is a great way to try out the Factom blockchain.

Building transparency in the mortgage industry

A blockchain document management service, Factom Harmony is the company's first commercial product. It's targeted for mortgage originators, the institutions that issue loans to consumers for homes.

Factom Harmony (shown in Figure 7-4) works by converting various imaging systems utilized by banks into a blockchain vault for documents. It creates and manages entries in real-time as the mortgage is processed. Then it secures a record of the data within Factom, allowing metadata to be shared transparently and points to confidential data between trusted parties.

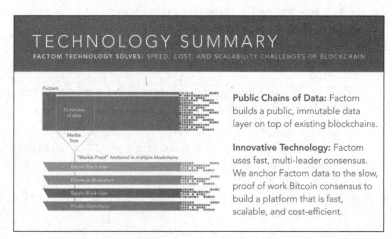

FIGURE 7-4: Factom Harmony.

Illustration courtesy of Factom, Inc.

In simple terms, Factom Harmony is a document catalog that sits on an imaging system. It's a radical improvement over the existing systems because individuals who get involved years later can be sure that the records they're handed are identical to the ones that originated the loan. No longer do mortgage buyers need to trust the fastidiousness of the many intermediaries between origination and themselves.

Factom is hoping to capture some of the value that comes from eliminating costs associated with document assembly. Banks and other originators currently spend immense amounts of time ensuring audits and record reviews are only conducted using the correct set of records and data. This often breaks down when multiple stakeholders coordinate while interacting with loan documents across disparate sources.

Securing data on the blockchain: The digital vault

Factom Harmony (see the preceding section) provides the ability to store the specific data and documents, used for decision and compliance, to a permanent blockchain, while at the same time sharing that data with any party that needs it. Data that has been stored within this system has a clear version history. Missing data is also evident. It was designed for scenarios like audits, lawsuits, foreclosures, loan trading, securitization, and regulatory reviews.

Core technology limitations, during the decade leading up to the 2008 market crash, were focused on speed, throughput, checklist management, and document collection. The systems were not designed to collect records and the associated data in a manner that permanently preserves evidence of the decisions and actions.

Today's regulatory environment requires business to be far more diligent in their efforts to document and maintain the records and data associated with every decisions. Any deficiencies in the documentation of the process are often attributed to malice. Without the ability to perfectly preserve the evidence of the data and the decisions associated with it.

How Harmony works with Factom technology

Factom's technology is a combination of blockchain technology, digital signatures, and a set of cryptographic functions developed by the U.S. National Institute of Standards and Technology (NIST). A series of data points is preserved along with a cryptographic proof on other blockchains that allows users to preserve the data and documents for future use. This process creates an electronic catalog of files that can be accessed and validated at any time by any authorized parties.

Using the SHA-256 cryptographic function, Factom generates a hash of each document and data file stored within the Factom blockchain. The hash creates cryptographic proof that a file has never been altered or changed.

REMEMBER

A *hash* is a kind of "fingerprint" for a set of data that represents the contents of a file but without the risk of the data being exposed.

Additionally, Harmony generates and stores a set of key meta-data points along with the hash for every document and data file associated with the record. Within the metadata documents and data files are associated and linked using the same cryptographic tools. This metadata along with the file hashes is written to the Factom blockchain.

Using blockchain as a public witness

Factom creates multiple public witnesses for the data that it secures. Its blockchain is tiny in comparison to the behemoths such as Bitcoin and Ethereum. Their system does not have mining as part of the consensus mechanism. Currently, the system is not even producing any new tokens. The larger and more decentralized a blockchain, the more secure it is from a successful attack.

Mining cryptocurrency is what most public blockchains do to secure themselves. It's what incentives nodes to join the network.

Factom overcomes this obstacle with a clever method that gives it compounded security. It anchors the data placed in the Factom blockchain within Bitcoin and Ethereum. This is done every ten minutes through hashing. They take the full data set and hash it until there is only one hash that can represent the whole Factom blockchain. Doing so helps protect the protocol for things like 51 percent attacks.

Verifying physical documents: dLoc with Factom

Smartrac, the world's leading developer, manufacturer, and supplier of RFID transponders, inlays, prelaminates, and semifinished cards partnered with Factom. Out of this partnership, a new way of securing physical objects with blockchains was created. This product and service is called dLoc. dLoc was designed as a sticker that can be placed on almost anything. It has special utility for paper-based documents such as breeder documents.

dLoc is an end-to-end secure document management system that uses both hardware and software. dLoc's adhesive Smartrac encoded Near Field Communication (NFC) transponder sticker with an embedded chip is placed on documents or other goods and then secures them using the Factom blockchain.

TECHNICAL STUFF

NFC communication protocols allow two electronic devices, to establish connection when brought near each other.

By combining cloud-based software with Factom's technology, an immutable identity is created over time for just about anything. People with certain levels of clearance can access and validate the physical document using the dLoc mobile app.

dLoc also allows issuing agencies or entities to turn their offline documents into digital instances that can be easily connected to the existing digital systems and bridge the gap between the offline and online worlds. This solution can be applied to a broad range of documents such as birth certificates, land titles, court, and medical records.

dLoc represents the first practical document authentication system that uses the Factom blockchain to solve the data integrity gap between the physical and digital world. It's the first reliable way to secure information on paper-based documents with digital data using blockchain technology. dLoc's data and identity authentication solution hold great promise for both public and private sectors, where paper-based documents are widely used.

REMEMBER

dLoc does not eliminate fraud. People will be people and find ways to bypass, circumvent, and steal. This technology makes it much more challenging and costly to do so. At this point, someone can buy a new identity or forge goods almost anywhere. And in some cases, these identities are indistinguishable from authentic documents and commodities.

dLoc was created as a way to extend the impossibility of blockchain technology to physical objects and documents. They have also created a system that can notify you if your identity is being tampered with and the possibility of doing something about it.

Chapter **8**

Examining the EOS Blockchain

EOS is a newer blockchain, and its developers are hoping to scale the efforts pioneered by Ethereum. EOS is one of the most popular cryptocurrencies trading in markets. Block.one, the development company behind EOS, raised $4 billion during its year-long initial coin offering (ICO) in 2017. Like Ethereum, EOS allows its users to program smart contracts that can perform a wide range of functions.

The defining difference between EOS and Ethereum — and why you may want to learn more about the EOS system — is EOS's consensus algorithm. EOS has pioneered a new system called delegated proof-of-stake (DPOS). Token holders on the EOS blockchain may select block producers through voting. Anyone can potentially be a block producer as long as they can persuade token holders. If you've read Chapter 7 on Factom's consensus algorithm, this may sound familiar.

This chapter dives into the practical applications and future of the EOS blockchain and explains uses for its technology. Because EOS is a relatively newer blockchain, Block.one has yet to produce a user-friendly application, but it has a tremendous amount of resources for developers and may at some point have better resources for everyday users. Given its significant funding, you'd be wise to keep an eye on the project — it will most likely grow beyond any other project in the blockchain space.

Getting Familiar with EOS

The Cayman Island–based crypto company Block.one raised approximately 7.12 million Ether valued at the time at $4 billion via its ICO. Investors traded their Ether for the EOS token. Like most ICOs, in its ICO EOS used the Ethereum ERC20 as the mechanism for raising capital. You may find it funny to know that EOS has been called the "Ethereum killer," even though it needed Ethereum to get off the ground.

The promise of the EOS project was to provide its users with an experience similar to those currently offered by centralized services — the security and redundancy of blockchain technology at the cost and speed of the Amazon cloud. Most blockchain developers want to find ways to push down the prices that tend to go up with the number of users that their platforms attract, while increasing their transaction speed and capacity. For proof-of-work blockchains, the more users they have, the more it costs to use the blockchain as a service, and the slower the system.

In the first version of blockchain technology, the purpose was straightforward: Bitcoin enabled users to send cryptocurrency from one user to another, and the Bitcoin blockchain was used to keep track of ownership. Ethereum pioneered blockchain 2.0; it coupled the digital permanence and trustless architecture of Bitcoin with the ability to write code within a blockchain, enabling the creation of smart contracts. The developers behind the EOS software created a new blockchain architecture; it's blockchain 3.0, and it enables the vertical scaling of the number of transactions per second and horizontal scaling of the number of decentralized applications it can handle.

EOS takes both the transparent nature of blockchain technology and the ability to create smart contracts and adds account functionality, authentication, databases, asynchronous communication, and the scheduling of applications across many central processing unit (CPU) cores. The architecture of EOS may scale to millions of transactions per second, reduces user fees, and allow for easier deployment of decentralized applications (Dapps).

EOS directly confronts several of the core arguments that developers have had with previous blockchain systems:

>> Blockchain technology must be able to support tens of millions of active daily users, just like Google, Facebook, Twitter, and Amazon do every day, without increased cost or crashed systems.

>> Blockchain technology must be able to come down significantly in cost to host all the types of applications that could benefit from trustless systems.

A blockchain platform that is free to use will likely gain more widespread adoption.

» Blockchain software must allow for nonpolitical upgrades and bug recovery. Bitcoin and Ethereum have both been stalled in development due to infighting form the core developers and financial pressure from miners.

» Blockchain developers that are building applications need the versatility to enhance their applications with new features while still allowing the security of blockchain software.

» Blockchain software also needs to be fast and provide a good user experience. Long delays discourage user retention and make applications built on a blockchain less competitive.

The team at Block.one hopes to solve all these core issues that make blockchain software unattractive for commercial development through their decentralized consensus algorithm called DPOS. The DPOS algorithm empowers token holders to select block producers through a voting system.

The EOS DPOS produces blocks of transactions every 0.5 second. The blocks are produced in rounds of 126, with 21 elected producers creating six blocks each. All block producers can sign all blocks but not more than one with the same time-stamp or the same block height. When 15 block producers have signed, the block is deemed unchangeable. This structure allows a transaction to be confirmed within an average of 0.25 second. This is extremely fast for a blockchain technology.

If a block producer has committed to produce a block but fails to do so, then that producer is skipped, creating at least a 0.5-second gap in the EOS blockchain. If a block producer misses its block and has not produced any blocks within 24 hours, the producer is removed.

The nodes on the DPOS don't often fork their blockchain records because they aren't competing in the same sense as the nodes on proof-of-work blockchains such as Bitcoin. On EOS, they cooperate to produce blocks. When there is a fork, the DPOS consensus automatically switches to the longest chain. Block producers can do screwy stuff like producing blocks on two versions of the EOS blockchain (forks) at the same time. However, the theory behind EOS is that if a block producer is caught taking nonbeneficial action, it will be voted out. The EOS blockchain keeps cryptographic evidence of such double production to make it easy to see who's cheating.

WARNING

The scalability of EOS has drawbacks. Fewer nodes, only 21, maintaining the DPOS blockchain means that it's very centralized and has security risks.

New mining versus old mining

When Bitcoin began, a desktop computer could be used to mine. However, the increase in the hash rate for the Bitcoin blockchain soon consumed all the system resources of ordinary computers to keep up.

Blockchains that have reached the hash difficulty of gigahashes are beyond the capacity of your average computer. Even this rate can be prohibitive for many miners. It requires a lot of energy, time, and resources to be profitable. Because of the EOS DPOS algorithm, you can still use a standard computer to earn tokens.

Bitcoin miners discovered that they could adapt the graphical processing unit (GPU) in computer graphics cards to do mining. The GPU often gave miners over 50 times the speed advantage, and the GPU also consumed less electricity, so it was cheaper to run.

In 2011, mining farms started popping up. They used specialized equipment called field-programmable gate array (FPGA) processors. These devices attached to miners' computers using a USB port and used less power than CPU or GPU mining.

The best mining hardware now utilizes application-specific integrated circuit (ASIC). ASIC machines mine at extreme hashing speeds and, from my personal experience, they can be quite noisy. If you choose to buy one, take your time and read the reviews. Also, make sure it will have a reasonable payback time and be compatible with what you want to mine.

As blockchain software moves beyond proof-of-concept and into the mainstream, the idea of mining will have to change, too. EOS doesn't mine in the same sense that other blockchains do. It produces blocks, and the nodes that make the blocks are rewarded.

Technically, anyone can sign up, but given that there are only ever 21 elected block producers, it's difficult to win one of the coveted slots. You may be able to stake some of your EOS tokens with a prominent block producer and be rewarded for doing so. This works similarly to how you stake some tokens on the Waves platform (see Chapter 6).

The 21 block producers

Unlike Bitcoin, in which anyone can verify transactions and produce blocks, a select set of nodes maintains the EOS DPOS blockchain. As a participant and EOS token holder, you can vote on these nodes like a political election.

Elected nodes, called *EOS delegates,* are the only ones clearing transactions on EOS. There are just 21 delegates at any time and many backup delegates waiting in case one of the elected nodes goes down. The nodes with the most votes win the right to produce blocks. Some of the delegates will share their block rewards with the users who voted for them.

As a token holder, you can change your vote at any time. The theory is that this will discourage block producers from acting against the best interests of the community. Currently, voting or switching your vote isn't very intuitive. Nor is there yet a clear way for the average person to know if she should change her vote.

TIP

Greymass, an EOS block producer, has created a voting tool. This tool was designed by a third party so it isn't as secure as voting through your command-line interface. But Greymass's voting system is open source and supported by several competitive block producers.

The EOS system rewards block producers with new tokens. The EOS system creates 5 percent more tokens each year, increasing the overall supply. Of these new tokens, 0.25 percent go to block producers and 0.75 percent go to standby block producers; this is about 100 EOS for a day for qualified standby block producers. Four percent of the new global supply goes back into a pool used for EOS development and research. Worker proposals are presented to the community, and token holders vote on what improvements they want.

Setting Up EOS Voting for Block Producers

EOS tokens are available on most exchanges. You can trade some Bitcoin or Ethereum for EOS tokens on the Poloniex exchange at the time of writing this book. After you've purchased or exchanged some of your Bitcoin or Ethereum for EOS tokens, you'll qualify to vote. You'll need to set up a new EOS wallet now, too. Follow these steps:

1. **On your phone navigate to your app store.**

2. **Search for EOS Lynx.**

   The company webpage for EOS Lynx is at https://eoslynx.com.

3. **Download the wallet.**

   At the time of writing, there was a $0.99 charge for the EOS Lynx wallet.

4. **Choose an account name.**

   Your account name also is your wallet address. It must contain exactly 12 characters (numbers and letters only).

   TIP

   Pick something easy to remember — you may use your account name in the future much like an email address.

5. **Write down your private key.**

   Make sure to write down your private key and keep it in a secure place.

6. **Load your wallet with EOS tokens.**

   This is the wallet name and not an address like other blockchains

   You can buy or traded for them on exchanges such as Poloniex (www.poloniex.com) or Bitrex (www.bittrex.com).

Now that you have an EOS account and some EOS tokens, you're set to connect to Greymass for voting.

Setting up the Greymass voting tool

The Greymass app does a few very cool things. It lets you vote for block producers, transfer EOS to other accounts, and stake EOS tokens for CPU bandwidth. This gives you the right to resource usage on the network as a developer and conveys the weight of your votes.

Follow these steps to vote for a block producer on EOS:

1. **Navigate to Greymass's GitHub at** https://github.com/greymass/eos-voter.

2. **Download and install Greymass's voting tool for your operating system.**

3. **Click Connect to an API Node.**

4. **Enter your EOS wallet name.**

   This is the name of the wallet that you created in the previous section.

5. **Enter your EOS private key.**

   You can find your private key for your EOS wallet on the document you wrote it down on. Or you can look for it in the EOS Lynx wallet. It will be under Export Private Key and the icon on the left of your account name in the wallet.

6. **Enter a secure password.**

   Don't forget to write down the password and keep it in a safe and separately place from your private key.

Voting for a block producer

Now that you have Greymass set up, you can start voting. But before you get going, it's worth digging deeper into who to vote for to secure your records and applications. This is important on EOS because it doesn't use a proof-of-work model and instead relies on voting to keep the system honest. The block producers are the backbone of the infrastructure of EOS, and if they fail, then the system is vulnerable.

Inside the Greymass application, under Voting, you can see a list of all the block producer candidates. From this list, you can explore the candidate's websites and social media accounts. Look for a few key things that will help narrow your choice:

>> Do they have a website?

>> Do they have a positive track record in the community?

>> Do they share block rewards?

>> Do they have social media?

>> What is their contribution to the community?

>> Do they have a road map for development?

>> Do they have an email, Telegram.org channel, or another social channel for communication available?

>> What is their technical experience?

>> Do they have a positive track record in the community?

When you're ready to vote, follow these steps:

1. **Navigate to the Greymass application on your computer.**

   This is the application that you installed in the previous section.

2. **Click Producer Voting.**

   On the left side of the screen (Mac) or right side of the screen (PC), you see the list of block producer candidates.

3. **Browse through the candidates and take some time to read about them.**

4. **When you know who you want to vote for, click the icon to the right of the block producer's name.**

   The icon looks like a small box with a negative sign within it. You can select up to 30 block producers at a time, but you don't have to.

5. **Click Submit Votes for Selected Producers.**

Congratulations! You've voted and participated in the EOS blockchain!

Introducing the EOS Decentralized Application Collection

EOS has begun to spawn one of the largest Dapps collections on the Internet. Dapps are applications that are built on blockchains and take advantage of things like digital permanence, distribution, censorship resentence, and native cryptocurrencies. Many entrepreneurs have chosen to build their apps on EOS because it offers low latency and reduced cost over other blockchains.

Ethereum is still the most popular platform for building Dapps, but EOS may catch up soon as it continues to attract smart contract developers from other platforms. Another reason developers are migrating to EOS is that it uses a common programming languages such as WebAssembly (WASM; a web standard with support from Google, Microsoft, and Apple) and C++. With the significant capital that EOS has raised, it has been able to provide amazing developer tools and libraries.

You can have a look at all the newest applications being built on EOS by going to DappRadar at `https://dappradar.com/rankings/protocol/eos`.

Everipedia: The next-generation encyclopedia

Everipedia is an EOS blockchain version of the popular website Wikipedia. It's a wiki-based online encyclopedia that is censorship resistant and keeps a history of all edits to its pages. It uses its own native token called *IQ* to support content generation. Everipedia's creation predates EOS by a few years — it was founded all the way back in 2014 but migrated to EOS in 2018.

With a goal of creating the most accessible online encyclopedia, Everipedia is much easier to create content with than Wikipedia is. The Everipedia founder also took elements from traditional social media sites and has allowed celebrities to communicate with fans.

You can create pages on any topic. The pages must be cited and neutral because generating new pages is easy and doesn't have the same oversite as Wikipedia. You can imagine that, with the censorship resistance of blockchain, Everipedia could be abused and some content could be blatantly false. Everipedia offers a service that allows users to tailor pages and monitor them for updates and to prevent vandalism. Keep that in mind as you browse the site.

Follow these steps to create your very own page that is secured with the EOS blockchain:

1. **Navigate to Everipedia at** `https://everipedia.org`.

2. **Click Menu.**

3. **Click Log In/Register.**

   When you get to the registration page, pick your favorite social media site to log in with. As of this writing, Facebook, Twitter, and Scatter are available.

4. **Create a four-digit PIN.**

   Write down this PIN and keep it someplace safe.

5. **Click the plus sign (+)in the upper-left corner (Mac) or upper-right corner (PC).**

6. **Enter the name of the page you would like to create**

   As a suggestion, I created an author page for my technical editor, Scott Robinson: `https://everipedia.org/wiki/lang_en/the-scott-rob/`.

7. **Enter your content.**

   Don't forget to add an image and cite your work.

8. **Click Submit.**

Decentralized EOS games

Games stretch blockchain technology to its fullest. They create things like *sovereign identities* (an identity that the holder of the ID or document controls and proves validity through a blockchain entry). Blockchain games often also use things like *self-replicating digital assets* (digital goods that when combined in some way during gameplay can create a new asset); the crypto game Cryptokitties is an example of this type of asset. Games also often use tiny payments often called *microtransactions*. Games open up blockchain technology to the average user and all the potential that that holds.

The EOS blockchain is now powering many new games. EOS is an attractive option because it has built-in functionality that allows for new types of games. Blockchains, by nature, are censorship resistant. Not only can anyone play but it's difficult to prevent a game from operating globally. Some types of games may not be legal in your region (for example, gambling is often prohibited or heavily regulated).

Blockchains also allow for digital ownership that moves beyond the standards of centralized game corporations. Instead of a corporation owning and controlling your in-game assets like skins for your avatar, the assets are controlled by you. Blockchains also have native money or, rather, a cryptocurrency that makes it easy to facilitate payments and reduce chargebacks from users. This feature is attractive for developers. Also, the fee structure for processing transaction on blockchains can be cheaper than using credit card processors.

EOS has started to become the blockchain of choice for game development because of its high speed and low transaction cost. This means that the smart contracts (also known as chain code) can run faster and cheaper on EOS — a very important consideration for game development.

TIP

DappRadar is a great place to check out the latest games on EOS: `https://dappradar.com/rankings/protocol/eos/category/games`.

WARNING

Blockchain technology doesn't have some of the benefits of centralized services. If a game breaks, there is no customer support. If you lose your assets, they're gone forever. Plus, if another player is behaving unfairly, there isn't much that can be done. Blockchain technology is still the Wild West, and games bring out the competition, ego, and greed.

3

Powerful Blockchain Platforms

IN THIS PART . . .

Ascertain the largest business blockchain consortium, Hyperledger, and what benefits and impact it will have for your industry and organization.

Understand Microsoft's blockchain efforts and core tools available to you through its network offerings.

Evaluate the IBM Bluemix project and the implications of blockchain technology combined with artificial intelligence.

Chapter 9

Getting Your Hands on Hyperledger

yperledger is a foundation that supports a community of software developers and technology enthusiasts who are building industry standards for blockchain frameworks and platforms. Hyperledger's work is crucial because they're creating blockchain technology that fit the needs of businesses. Cryptocurrencies on public blockchains have regulatory implications and liabilities that prevent many companies from utilizing these networks. Hyperledger has many of the same benefits of public blockchain technology but operates without a cryptocurrency. With big supporters such as Intel and IBM, Hyperledger is the "trusted" deployment platform for enterprise teams.

Hyperledger and its unique project are growing every day. As of this writing, it has more than 100 member companies and several blockchain applications in incubation. Hyperledger's first few projects include Fabric, Iroha, and Sawtooth. These are frameworks that developers can use to build private blockchains, create smart contracts, and build distributed identity for people and things.

In this chapter, I explain how to create an asset tracking and a smart auction application using Hyperledger's Composer tool. I also introduce you to the Fabric, Iroha, and Sawtooth projects. You gain a deep understanding of what the future of commercialized blockchain will hold for your company and industry. This knowledge will help you as you explore which technologies to utilize and which to avoid, saving you development time and resources.

Getting to Know Hyperledger

At the end of 2015, the Linux Foundation formed the Hyperledger project to develop an enterprise-grade and open-source distributed ledger framework. They hoped to focus the blockchain community on building robust, industry-specific applications, platforms, and hardware systems to support businesses.

The Linux Foundation saw that there were many different groups building blockchain technology without a cohesive direction. The industry was duplicating effort, and the tribalism was leading teams to solve the same problem twice. The foundation members saw similarities between the birth of the Internet and the emergence of blockchain technology: If blockchain was going to realize its fullest potential, an open-source and collaborative development strategy was desperately needed.

The Hyperledger project is led by Executive Director Brian Behlendorf, who has decades of experience dating back to the original Linux Foundation and Apache Foundation, as well as being a chief technology officer (CTO) of the World Economic Forum. So, it's not surprising that Hyperledger has been well received. Many of the top business and industry leaders have joined the project, including Accenture, Cisco, Fujitsu Limited, IBM, Intel, J.P. Morgan, and Wells Fargo. It has also attracted many of the top blockchain organizations.

Hyperledger's technical steering committees ensure robustness and interoperability between these different technologies. The hope is that the cross-industry, open-source collaboration will advance blockchain technology and deliver billions of dollars in economic value by sharing the costs of research and development across many organizations.

Hyperledger is identifying and addressing the critical features and requirements missing from the blockchain technology ecosystem. It's also fostering a cross-industry open standard for distributed ledgers and holding open space for developers to contribute to building better blockchain systems.

Hyperledger has a project life cycle similar to that of the Linux Foundation. A proposal is submitted, and then the accepted proposals are brought into incubation. When a project has reached a stable state, it graduates and is moved into an active state. As of yet, all Hyperledger projects are in the proposal or incubation stage. Each of the projects is led by a large corporation or startup. For example, Fabric is led by IBM, Sawtooth by Intel, and Iroha by the startup Soramitsu.

TIP

Hyperledger, like many open-source projects, uses GitHub (www.github.com/hyperledger) and Slack (https://slack.hyperledger.org) to connect with teams working on each of the projects. These are great places to get the latest updates and to check on the progress that these projects are making in development.

Identifying Key Hyperledger Projects

Hyperledger has several revolutionary projects under incubation. In this section, I fill you in on the three most prominent and well-developed projects. These blockchain technologies include distributed ledger frameworks, smart contract engines, client libraries, graphical interfaces, utility libraries, and sample applications.

Focusing on Fabric

Fabric was the first blockchain implementation on Hyperledger. It has become the foundation for developing most blockchain applications. Fabric is unique within the blockchain ecosystem because it allows developers to use pieces of Fabric without committing to all the functionality — a truly tailored plug-and-play experience. Fabric also can create smart contracts called *chaincode*.

Fabric is a permissioned blockchain and does not utilize a cryptocurrency. This means that all the participants are known (as opposed to on a typical public blockchain where all the participants are anonymous by default). Fabric works like most blockchains in that it keeps a ledger of digital events. These events are structured as transactions and shared among the different participants. The transactions are executed without a cryptocurrency (in contrast, a public blockchain uses its native cryptocurrency to pay the network to operate and to allow all the participants to remain anonymous). To dive deeper into the subject of Fabric, go to https://trustindigitallife.eu/wp-content/uploads/2016/07/marko_vukolic.pdf.

All transactions are secured, private, and confidential. Fabric preserves its integrity by only allowing updates by consensus of the participants. When records have been inputted, they can never be altered.

Fabric is an enterprise solution interested in scalability and complying with regulations. All participants must register proof of identity to membership services to gain access to the system. Fabric issues transactions with derived certificates that are unlinkable to the owning participant, thereby offering anonymity on the network. Also, the content of each transaction is encrypted to ensure only the intended participants can see the content.

Fabric has a modular architecture. You can add or take away components by implementing its protocol specification. Its container technology can handle most of the mainstream languages for smart contracts development.

Investigating the Iroha project

Hyperledger's Iroha project is building on the work completed in the Fabric project. It's meant to complement Fabric, Sawtooth Lake, and the other projects under

Hyperledger. Hyperledger added the Iroha project to incubation because the other projects didn't have any infrastructure projects written in C++. Not having a C++ project severely limited how many people could benefit from the work on Hyperledger and the number of developers who could contribute to the project.

Besides, most blockchain development at this point has been at the lowest infrastructure level, and there has been little to no development work on user interaction or mobile applications. Hyperledger believes that Iroha is necessary for the popularization of blockchain technology. This project fills the gap in the market by bringing in more developers and providing libraries for mobile user interface development.

At the time of this writing, Iroha is a very new project and has not integrated with Fabric or Sawtooth Lake. Hyperledger has plans to expand functionality to work with the other blockchain projects soon. Its iOS, Android, and JavaScript libraries will provide supportive functions like digitally signing transactions. It will be handy for commercial app development, and it will add new layers of security and business models only possible with blockchain technology.

Introducing Sumeragi: The new consensus algorithm

Blockchains have systems that allow them to first agree on a single version of the truth and then record that agreed-upon truth in their ledger. An agreement system is called a *consensus.* A consensus is complicated. Grasping the nuances of how and why consensuses act in the way they do is well beyond the scope of this book. It's also far more then you'll ever need as a business professional. What *does* matter for you are the consequences of different consensus mechanisms and how they affect what you're doing on that particular blockchain. I'm highlighting Iroha's consensus, Sumeragi, because it's very different from traditional blockchains.

Here are a few key things that make Sumeragi different:

>> **Sumeragi does not have a cryptocurrency.**

>> **Nodes that start consensus are added into the system by the Fabric member services.** Nodes build a reputation over time based on how they've interacted with the ledger. This is a permission blockchain run by known entities.

>> **New entries are added to the ledger in a unique way.** The first node that starts consensus, called the *leader,* broadcasts the entry to a group of other nodes; those nodes then validate. If they don't validate, the first node will rebroadcast after a predetermined duration of time.

Depending on your use case for blockchain, Iroha may be positive or negative. If you're worried about censorship, Iroha may not be right for you. In this case, you'll be better off looking at a blockchain that is censorship resistant. If you're worried about other players on the network committing arbitrage, Iroha may also not be right — further investigation is needed. If you want to know all the players in your blockchain, Iroha may be exactly what you're looking for.

Developing mobile apps

Skip this section if you aren't part of the app development space.

Iroha is built for the web and mobile app developers so they can access the strengths of the Hyperledger systems. The Iroha team saw that having a distributed ledger wasn't useful if there were no applications utilizing it.

Iroha has a development path for the following encapsulated C++ components:

>> Sumeragi consensus library

>> Ed25519 digital signature library

>> SHA-3 hashing library

>> Iroha transaction serialization library

>> P2P broadcast library

>> API server library

>> iOS library

>> Android library

>> JavaScript library

>> Blockchain explorer/data visualization suite

One of the major hurdles of the blockchain industry has been in making systems user-friendly. Iroha has created open-source software libraries for iOS, Android, and JavaScript and made common application programming interface (API) functions convenient to call. It's still early in development, but Iroha is a good resource to explore for business use cases.

Diving into Sawtooth Lake

Sawtooth Lake by Intel is another distributed ledger project in Hyperledger. It's focused on being a highly modular platform for building new distributed ledgers for companies.

As of this writing, the release version has software that is only *simulating* the consensus. It doesn't provide security for your project and should only be utilized for testing out new ideas.

Sawtooth Lake does not operate with a cryptocurrency. It maintains the security of the platform by allowing businesses to create private blockchains. These businesses running private blockchains then share the burden of computational requirements of the network. In its documentation, Sawtooth Lake states that this type of setup will ensure universal agreement on the state of the shared ledger.

Sawtooth Lake has taken the basic model of blockchains and turned it on its head. Most blockchains have three elements:

>> A shared record of the current state of the blockchain

>> A way of inputting new data

>> A way of agreeing on that data

Sawtooth Lake merges the first two into a signal process it calls a *transaction family.* This model is best in use cases where all the participating parties have a mutual benefit to having a correct record.

Intel has allowed its software to be flexible enough to accommodate custom transaction families that reflect the unique requirements of each business. It also built three templates for building digital assets:

>> **EndPointRegistry:** A place to record items in a blockchain

>> **IntegerKey:** A shared ledger that is used for supply chain management

>> **MarketPlace:** A blockchain trading platform for buying, selling, and trading digital assets

Exploring the consensus algorithm: Proof of Elapsed Time

The consensus algorithm for Sawtooth Lake is called Proof of Elapsed Time (PoET). It was built to run in a secure area of the main processor of your computer, called a *trusted execution environment* (TEE). PoET leverages the security of the TEE to prove that time has passed by time-stamping transactions.

Other consensus algorithms have some kind of time-stamping element as well. The way they ensure that the records have not been changed is through publicly publishing their blockchains as proof that they have not been altered. The published ledger acts as a public witness that anyone can roll back and check. It's sort of like publishing an ad in a newspaper to prove something happened.

PoET also has a lottery system that works a bit differently from other blockchains using proof of work. It randomly selects a node from the pool of validating nodes.

The probability of a node being selected increases proportionally to how much processing resources that node contributed to the shared ledger. Measures may be put in place to prevent nodes from gaming the system and corrupting the ledger.

Deploying Sawtooth

Intel has put together some fantastic documentation and tutorials at `https://intelledger.github.io/tutorial.html`. There, Intel walks you through the process of setting up a virtual development environment for a blockchain, and it even has one for building a blockchain Tic-Tac-Toe game. You need to be familiar with Vagrant and VirtualBox in order to take advantage of what Intel has to offer.

TIP

You may also want to review *Coding For Dummies*, by Nikhil Abraham (Wiley), prior to trying these tutorials.

Building Your System in Fabric

A lot of work has gone into making Fabric accessible. The Hyperledger Composer is an easy-to-use tool that allows you to create blockchain application proof of concepts (POCs). The best part is that it will enable you to define your business network with JavaScript, one of the most popular development languages in the world. This feature alone will significantly cut down on your need for specialized blockchain developers.

The Hyperledger Composer will decrease the development time and cost and allow you to be production ready sooner. Another benefit of the Composer is that it utilizes LoopBacks. LoopBacks communicates digital data streams back to your existing business system, keeping your operations in sync. You still need a good development team to do this, but you can easily mock up your business logic.

TECHNICAL
STUFF

A LoopBack is a bit of code that sits in your software and communicates a digital data stream back to a source without intentional processing or modification.

Building asset tracking with Hyperledger Composer

You can try the Hyperledger Composer in your browser without needing to download any special software. The Composer also has a download option that works great if you need to work offline or need to use the Composer's full application development capabilities.

For this quick tutorial, you need a web browser and an Internet connection. In the following sections, I show you how to deploy your own network, set up a tracking demo, and move assets from one location to another. It's mostly a point-and-click demo, but you also need to copy and paste a few snippets of code.

You'll use the Animal Tracking Business Network framework. It was built as a use case for the UK government and farmers. In this demo, a farmer can move animals between fields, and the UK regulator can track the locations of the cows. The assets in this demo happen to be animals, but they could represent any type of object that needs to have its location tracked by a third party, such as a regulator or insurance provider.

Step 1: Setting up a tracking network

The first step is to set up a tracking network. Follow these steps:

1. **Go to the Hyperledger Composer website at** `https://composer-playground.mybluemix.net/login.`

2. **Click Deploy a New Business Network.**

3. **Name your network** animal-tracking.

4. **Enter a description for the network**

5. **Give the network an admin card to be created.**

6. **Select your business network project under samples on npm animaltracking-network.**

7. **Click Deploy.**

Step 2: Setting up a test demo

After you've set up a tracking network, you're ready to set up a test demo. Follow these steps:

1. **Open a second browser tab.**

2. **Copy and paste the URL from your first tab into the second tab.**

3. **On your first tab, click Define.**

4. **On your second tab, click Test.**

5. **Open the Define window.**

6. Copy this command:

```
{
"$class": "com.biz.SetupDemo"
}
```

7. Open the Test window.

8. Click All Transactions.

9. Click Submit Transaction.

10. Select SetupDemo from the pull-down menu.

11. Paste this command:

```
{
"$class": "com.biz.SetupDemo"
}
```

12. Click Submit.

Step 3: Moving your cow

In this section, you digitally track the movement of your asset from one location to another. Often assets move location, and it's beneficial to allow other people you collaborate with to know where they are at any given time.

1. Open the Define window.

2. Copy this command:

```
{
"$class": "com.biz.AnimalMovementDeparture",
"fromField": "resource:com.biz.Field#FIELD_1",
"animal": "resource:com.biz.Animal#ANIMAL_1",
"from": "resource:com.biz.Business#BUSINESS_1",
"to": "resource:com.biz.Business#BUSINESS_2"
}
```

3. Open the Test window.

4. Click All Transactions.

5. Select AnimalMovementDeparture.

6. Paste this command:

```
{
"$class": "com.biz.AnimalMovementDeparture",
"fromField": "resource:com.biz.Field#FIELD_1",
```

```
"animal": "resource:com.biz.Animal#ANIMAL_1",
"from": "resource:com.biz.Business#BUSINESS_1",
"to": "resource:com.biz.Business#BUSINESS_2"
}
```

7. Click Submit.

Step 4: Receiving your cow

In this section, you complete the transfer of the asset by accepting its new location. This is a double-entry feature that allows for accountability among team members.

1. Open the Define window.

2. Copy this command:

```
{
"$class": "com.biz.AnimalMovementArrival",
"arrivalField": "resource:com.biz.Field#FIELD_2",
"animal": "resource:com.biz.Animal#ANIMAL_1",
"from": "resource:com.biz.Business#BUSINESS_1",
"to": "resource:com.biz.Business#BUSINESS_2"
}
```

3. Open the Test window.

4. Click All Transactions.

5. Select AnimalMovementDeparture.

6. Paste this command:

```
{
"$class": "com.biz.AnimalMovementArrival",
"arrivalField": "resource:com.biz.Field#FIELD_2",
"animal": "resource:com.biz.Animal#ANIMAL_1",
"from": "resource:com.biz.Business#BUSINESS_1",
"to": "resource:com.biz.Business#BUSINESS_2"
}
```

7. Click Submit.

Congratulations! You've now documented the movement of your cow from one location to another on a platform that a third party can use to verify the location and identity of that animal.

Working with Smart Contracts on Hyperledger

A *smart contract* is computer code that is written inside a blockchain protocol. Smart contracts are created to facilitate, verify, or enforce the prenegotiated terms between two or more parties. The blockchain protocol takes the place of enforcement of contracts. Smart contracts, in effect, allow two or more parties to work together without trust or the need to have authoritative judgment or settlement if things go wrong. At least that's how they work in theory. Many different platforms enable smart contracts. On Hyperledger, they're called chaincode.

Chaincode is conveniently written in Go, node.js, and Java and runs in a secured Docker container. Unlike other smart contract platforms that must expose your contract to a public network to enforce them, chaincode is isolated from the endorsing peer process of public blockchains. This allows you to keep your business logic private.

Another feature that distinguishes chaincode from many other platforms is that each chaincode contract is isolated. Other organizations using Hyperledger can't access your chaincode directly unless permissioned. This feature may reduce attack vectors on your contracts by keeps third parties from accessing them.

A *smart auction* is a type of smart contract. Its function is to transfer ownership of an item after predetermined parameters of the agreement are met. In this demo, you're going to create an auction for cars. You'll list assets for sale, set a reserve price, and test what happens when assets have met or exceeded their price at the end of the auction.

Because you're going to be using Hyperledger Composer, you don't need coding experience to complete this demo. You also don't need to download any special software. A Chrome browser and a good Internet connection will be enough.

Step 1: Setting up an auction network

To set up an auction network, follow these steps:

1. **Go to the Hyperledger Composer website at** `https://composer-playground.mybluemix.net/login`.
2. **Click carauction-network under the Samples on NPM section.**
3. **Click Connect Now on the carauction-network.**

Step 2: Setting up auction windows

To set up an auction window, follow these steps:

1. **Open a second browser tab.**
2. **Copy and paste the URL from your first tab into the second browser tab.**
3. **On your first tab, click Define.**
4. **On your second tab, click Test.**

Step 3: Creating an auctioneer

To create an auctioneer, follow these steps:

1. **Open the Define window.**
2. **Copy this command:**

```
{
"$class": "org.acme.vehicle.auction.Auctioneer",
"email": "auction@acme.org",
"firstName": "Jenny",
"lastName": "Jones"
}
```

3. **Open the Test window.**
4. **Click Create New Participant.**
5. **Paste this command:**

```
{
"$class": "org.acme.vehicle.auction.Auctioneer",
"email": "auction@acme.org",
"firstName": "Jenny",
"lastName": "Jones"
}
```

6. **Click Create New.**

Step 4: Creating two participants

To create two participants, follow these steps:

1. **Open the Define window.**

2. **Copy this command:**

```
{
"$class": "org.acme.vehicle.auction.Member",
"balance": 5000,
"email": "memberA@acme.org",
"firstName": "Amy",
"lastName": "Williams"
}
```

3. **Open the Test window.**

4. **Click Member.**

5. **Click Create New Participant.**

6. **Paste this command:**

```
{
"$class": "org.acme.vehicle.auction.Member",
"balance": 5000,
"email": "memberA@acme.org",
"firstName": "Amy",
"lastName": "Williams"
}
```

7. **Click Create New.**

8. **Repeat steps 1 through 6 for the second participant.**

Step 5: Creating a new asset

To create a new asset, follow these steps:

1. **Open the Define window.**

2. **Copy this command:**

```
{
"$class": "org.acme.vehicle.auction.Vehicle",
"vin": "vin:1234",
"owner":
    "resource:org.acme.vehicle.auction.
    Member#memberA@acme.org"
}
```

3. **Open the Test window.**

4. **Click Vehicle.**

5. **Click Create New Asset.**

6. **Paste this command:**

```
{
"$class": "org.acme.vehicle.auction.Vehicle",
"vin": "vin:1234",
"owner":
    "resource:org.acme.vehicle.auction.Member#memberA@
    acme.org"
}
```

7. **Click Create New.**

Step 6: Creating a new listing

To create a new listing, follow these steps:

1. **Open the Define window.**

2. **Copy this command:**

```
{
"$class": "org.acme.vehicle.auction.VehicleListing",
"listingId": "listingId:ABCD",
"reservePrice": 3500,
"description": "Arium Nova",
"state": "FOR_SALE",
"vehicle":
    "resource:org.acme.vehicle.auction.Vehicle#vin:1234"
}
```

3. **Open the Test window.**

4. **Click VehicleListing.**

5. **Click Create New Asset.**

6. **Paste this command:**

```
{
"$class": "org.acme.vehicle.auction.VehicleListing",
"listingId": "listingId:ABCD",
"reservePrice": 3500,
"description": "Arium Nova",
"state": "FOR_SALE",
```

```
"vehicle":
    "resource:org.acme.vehicle.auction.Vehicle#vin:1234"
}
```

7. **Click Create New.**

Congratulations! You've now created a smart auction, listed a car for sale, and created the three parties needed to execute the contract. Now that everything is all set to go, you're going to trigger the smart auction and transfer the car from owner to buyer.

Step 7: Auctioning off the car

To auction off the car, follow these steps:

1. **Open the Define window.**

2. **Copy this command:**

```
{

"$class": "org.acme.vehicle.auction.Offer",
"bidPrice": 3500,
"listing":
    "resource:org.acme.vehicle.auction.VehicleListing#listing
    Id:ABCD",
"member":
    "resource:org.acme.vehicle.auction.Member#memberB@
    acme.org"
}
```

3. **Open the Test window.**

4. **Click Submit Transaction.**

5. **Select Offer from the pull-down menu.**

6. **Paste this command:**

```
{

"$class": "org.acme.vehicle.auction.Offer",
"bidPrice": 3500,
"listing":
    "resource:org.acme.vehicle.auction.VehicleListing#listing
    Id:ABCD",
```

```
"member":
    "resource:org.acme.vehicle.auction.Member#memberB@
    acme.org"
}
```

7. Click Submit.

Step 8: Closing your auction

To close your auction, follow these steps:

1. **Open the Define window.**

2. **Copy this command:**

```
{
"$class": "org.acme.vehicle.auction.CloseBidding",
"listing":
    "resource:org.acme.vehicle.auction.VehicleListing#listing
    Id:ABCD"
}
```

3. **Open the Test window.**

4. **Click Submit Transaction.**

5. **Select CloseBidding from the pull-down menu.**

6. **Paste this command:**

```
{
"$class": "org.acme.vehicle.auction.CloseBidding",
"listing":
    "resource:org.acme.vehicle.auction.VehicleListing#listing
    Id:ABCD"
}
```

7. **Click Submit.**

You've created a smart auction, listed an asset for sale, created a buyer, and sold the asset. Not bad! To learn more check out the Hyperledger community found at `https://hyperledger.github.io/composer/latest/support/support-index.html`.

Chapter **10**

Applying Microsoft Azure

I n this chapter, you get a preview of the exciting innovations that are taking place inside of Microsoft's Azure platform and how these changes can improve your business's efficiency and create new opportunities for products and services.

This chapter helps you compete for, collaborate with, and service customers in a global economy. Blockchain technology is opening new markets and changing business models. Microsoft is working hard to make it an assessable technology for traditional business.

This chapter also explains innovative blockchain bridges that are being built to allow you to connect and scale your existing systems. You find out how to deploy your own blockchain inside Azure and the keys elements to making a safe and hassle-free transition to blockchain systems for your business.

Bletchley: The Modular Blockchain Fabric

Project Bletchley concentrates on offering architectural building blocks for enterprise customers within a *consortium blockchain ecosystem* (a members-only, permissioned networks for members to execute contracts). Bletchley's blockchain fabric platform is powered by Azure, the cloud computing platform for Microsoft. Project Bletchley addresses the following:

>> Digital identity

>> Private key management

>> Customer privacy

>> Data security

>> Operations administration

>> System interoperability

In Project Bletchley, Azure provides the cloud layer for blockchain, serving as the platform where applications can be built and delivered. It will be availability in 24 regions globally. Azure is combining its traditional products such as hybrid cloud capabilities, extensive compliance certification portfolio, and enterprise-grade security to various blockchains. Microsoft wants to make it easier for the existing clients to quickly adopt blockchain technology, especially in controlled industries such as healthcare, financial services, and government.

Figure 10-1 shows project Bletchley's Blockstack Core v14, a new decentralized web of server-less applications where users can control their data.

Azure will work with several blockchain protocols. They are part of Hyperledger project and unspent transaction output (UTXO)–based protocols. This means that the Azure platform doesn't utilize a cryptocurrency and may be more appealing to enterprise customers. They'll also have integrations with more sophisticated pro-tocols, including Ethereum, that do utilize a cryptocurrency to secure the network.

Cryptlets for encrypting and authenticating

Project Bletchley is built around two ideas:

>> **Blockchain middleware:** Cloud storage, identity management, analytics, and machine learning

>> **Cryptlets:** Secure execution for interoperation and communication between Microsoft Azure, Bletchley's ecosystem, and your own technology

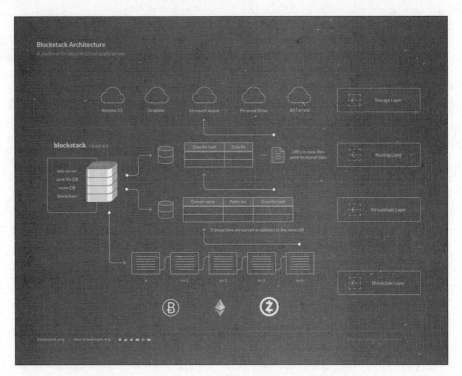

FIGURE 10-1:
Blockstack
Core v14.

Cryptlets are built as off-chaincode components, written in any language, executed within a trusted container, and communicated over a secure channel. Cryptlets can be used in smart contracts and UTXO systems, when additional functionality or information is needed.

Cryptlets bridge the gap in security between on- and off-chain execution of programs, operating when additional secure information is needed. They're what lets your customer relationship management (CRM) or trading platform connect with your cloud storage and then be secured with Ethereum, for example.

Bletchley's middleware works in tandem with Cryptlets and existing Azure services, like Active Directory and Key Vault, and other blockchain ecosystem technologies, to deliver a complete solution and ensure the reliable operation of your blockchain integration.

Table 10-1 shows the difference between an oracle and a Cryptlet. from the Devcon 2 presentation on Bletchley.

TABLE 10-1 Cryplets vs. Oracles

	Cryptlets	Oracles
Verification requirements	Requires trust with verification with a trusted host (HTTPS), a trusted Cryptlet key, and a trusted enclave signature.	Requires trust but no formal verification.
Infrastructure	Standard infrastructure. You achieve hardware-based isolation and attestation via enclaves available globally in Azure. Bletchley Cryptlet software development kit (SDK) frameworks (Utility and Contract) are available to help you get started quickly creating and consuming Cryptlets.	Customized infrastructure. You can write and host separately. Establishing trust is difficult. Oracles have been platform specific, and documentation is currently very sparse.
Developer use	Many language options are available, and they are blockchain agnostic.	Tied to their own blockchain and few language options.
Marketplace availability	A marketplace is available for publishing and discovery.	No common marketplace is available for publishing and discovery.

Cryptlets are built by developers and sold in Bletchley's marketplace. They address many different functionality sets that are essential to building distributed ledger–based applications. The market is growing to meet the demands of customers who need the necessary functionality, such as secure execution, integration, privacy, management, interoperability, and a full set of data services.

Utility and Contract Cryptlets and CrytoDelegates

There are two types of Cryptlets:

>> **Utility:** Utility Cryptlets provide encryption, timestamping, external data access, and authentication. They create a more sound and trusted transactions.

>> **Contract:** Contract Cryptlets are full delegation engines. They can function as autonomous agents or bots. They provide all the execution logic that a smart contract normally does but outside of a blockchain.

Contract Cryptlets are tied to smart contracts and are created when your smart contract is published. They run in parallel with your virtual machine and have greater performance over traditional smart contracts built inside blockchains because they don't require a mining fee to execute your contract. They're most attractive to noncryptocurrency blockchains users where chaincode and smart contracts are signed by known parties.

Figure 10-2 shows a depiction of a Cryplet container and the secure communication path to your smart contract.

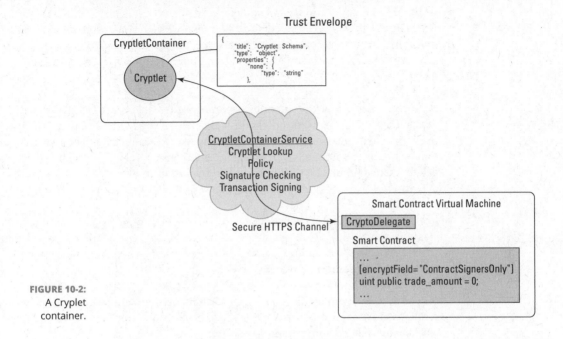

CryptoDelegates allow Utility and Contract Cryplets to function. They act as adaptors by creating functional hooks in your smart contract virtual machines. They call the Cryptlet from the code of your smart contract, which in turn creates a secure and authentic envelope for transactions.

Building in the Azure Ecosystem

Azure is a digital ecosystem and cloud computing platform. It connects enterprises directly with their cloud partners and SaaS. This, in turn, allows enterprises to transfer their data in an interconnected, reliable, and secure way.

The Azure cloud platform is the second largest Infrastructure as a Service (IaaS) platform in the world. It's a reliable and safe haven for your cloud computing and data storage. In Azure, there is a service known as ExpressRoute, which provides consumers a way to directly connect to Azure. This, in turn, prevents the performance and security issues that are widely seen in the public Internet.

In 2015, Microsoft decided to expand its Azure ecosystem using the Ethereum and Hyperledger blockchain systems. The first offering of Azure Blockchain as a Service is powered by Ethereum. Ethereum is a Turing-complete blockchain framework for build applications, and you can read about it in depth in Chapter 5 or in *Ethereum For Dummies,* by Michael G. Solomon (Wiley). Microsoft aims to build more offerings based on the blockchain technology and Hyperledger. It's also growing the Azure marketplace, while transitioning to a portal for customers on Azure.

Microsoft's Azure Stack program incorporates Azure Quickstart Templates, which deploy the various Azure resources with the help of the Azure Resource Manager in order to help you get more work done. The Azure Resource Manger allows customers to work with their business resources as a group. It enables them to deploy, delete, or update all the resources in their solution in a coordinated and single operation.

Azure Quickstart Templates can work for various environments, like production, staging, and testing. Through Azure Resource Manager, customers get several features for tagging, auditing, and security. These features help consumers to manage their resources after deployment.

Microsoft's Project Bletchley is their blockchain architecture that is merged with established enterprise technologies they were already offering. It gives Azure a blockchain backend and marketplace.

Bletchley's ecosystem is an approach taken by Microsoft in order to bring forward blockchain or distributed ledger networks to a wider audience in a safe and effective manner. They want to help build authentic solutions and address actual business problems.

CHOOSING YOUR TEMPLATE

The Quickstart Template is a tool that is designed to make it easier for the users of Project Bletchley to spin up a private blockchain group. Currently there are about a dozen blockchain templates that allow you spin up blockchain applications in Azure. In the future, more templates will become available.

The Ethereum private version is one of the best at automating the process. step-it is a step-by-step process where you can select the members of the your consortium, determine the number of nodes each user will have on the network, and then geographically distribute those nodes using the Azure cloud to boost resilience.

Getting Started with Chain on Azure

Chain, which provides blockchain technology solutions, released its Chain Core Developer Edition on Azure. Chain Core Developer Edition is an open-source and free version of the company's distributed ledger platform. It enables you to issue as well as transfer assets on authorized blockchain networks.

Through its test net, your developers can join or start a blockchain network, access in-depth technical tutorials and documentation, and build financial applications. They can also run their own prototypes on the Chain's test net or create their own personal network on Azure.

Installing Chain's distributed ledger

Chain Core Developer Edition accompanies code samples, a Java SDK, and getting-started guides. In addition, it comes with a dashboard interface and installers for Linux, Mac, and Windows.

Follow these steps to install your Chain Core Developer Edition:

1. **Navigate to Chain's install page at** https://chain.com/docs/core/get-started/install.

2. **Choose your operating system from the list.**

3. **Click Download.**

4. **Open the Chain program.**

5. **Run the Chain Core installer.**

Chain has an SDK available that gives you and your developer the software development tools that allows the creation of blockchain applications and assets.

Creating your own private network

You can create a private Ethereum Consortium Blockchain network in Azure. You should be able to do this on your own without the help of a developer. Just follow these steps:

1. **Sign up for or log into your Azure account.**

   There is a free trial option and a pay-as-you-go option that make it easy to try out Azure.

2. **Go to** `https://goo.gl/YtqnKa`.

3. **Click Deploy to Azure.**

Azure Resource Manager templates are created by members of the Azure community. Microsoft doesn't screen for security, compatibility, or performance.

4. **Complete the form.**

5. **Click Purchase.**

Congratulations! You now have a private Ethereum Consortium Blockchain network.

Using financial services on Azure's Chain

Chain launched its open-source and free developer platform. It includes a test network, which is operated by Microsoft, Chain, and the Initiative for Cryptocurrencies and Contracts (3CI). 3CI is the platform launched by Chain, which provides blockchain technology solutions and is Chain Core Developer Edition.

This platform enables you to issue as well as transfer assets on authenticated blockchain networks. It's an effort among leading financial companies and Chain. Various financial applications can be developed via Chain Core.

Many new innovative products are planned to be launched on this platform. The range covers payments, banking, insurance, and capital markets. Additionally, Visa has partnered with Chain in order to develop a secure, fast, and simple way to process business-to-business (B2B) payments worldwide.

Deploying Blockchain Tools on Azure

Azure has several other useful implementations of blockchain technology and tools that you might find useful. I cover four of Azure's core blockchain tools and projects in this section, including its Ethereum implementation; Cortana, an analytics machine learning tool; Azure's data visualization tool, Power BI; and its Active Directory (AD) tool. The last three are not specifically blockchain tools, but they can be used with your Azure blockchain project.

This section gives you an idea of what you can build with Azure and some of the tools available to make your project a success.

Exploring Ethereum on Azure

Ethereum Blockchain is now available as a service on Microsoft's Azure platform. This initiative is offered by ConsenSys and Microsoft in partnership. Solidity is a new project that they created that allows you to start building your decentralized application on Ethereum. Find out more at `https://marketplace.visualstudio.com/items?itemName=ConsenSys.Solidity`.

Ethereum Blockchain as a Service (EBaaS) enables enterprise developers and clients to develop a blockchain environment on the cloud and can be spun up with one click.

When you're deploying Ethereum blockchain on Azure, Azure offers two tools initially:

>> **BlockApps:** A semiprivate and private Ethereum blockchain environment

>> **Ether.Camp:** A built-in developer environment

BlockApps can also be deployed into the public environment of Ethereum. These tools allow rapid development of applications based on a smart contract.

Ethereum is a flexible and open system, which can be customized to meet the varied needs of customers. Read more about Ethereum in Chapter 5.

Cortana: Your analytics machine learning tool

Cortana is a powerful analytics machine learning tool based on cloud systems. It's a fully managed cloud service that enables users to easily and quickly build, organize, and share predictive analytics solutions. It provides many benefits to consumers.

By reviewing the analytics provided by Cortana Intelligence, you can take action sooner than your competitors by predicting the next big thing. This flexible and fast software allows you to build quick solutions for your industry, which are tailored to your particular needs.

Furthermore, the Cortana learning tool is secure and scalable. Cortana offers data value, irrespective of the complexity and size of the data. And, most of all, Cortana allows you to interact with smart agents, so that you can get closer to your consumers in more natural, practical, and useful ways. The Cortana Intelligence Suite is helpful in various sectors, including manufacturing, financial services, retail, and healthcare.

Visualizing your data with Power BI

Power BI, which is offered by Microsoft, is a powerful service based on the cloud system. It covers the latest business intelligence services and tools of Microsoft. This service assists data scientists in envisioning and sharing insights from the data of their organizations.

The Power BI data visualization course, which is provided online by edX, is part of the Microsoft Professional Program Certificate in Data Science. This cloud-based service is rapidly gaining popularity among data science professionals.

Power BI helps you to visualize and connect your data. In this course, students learn how to connect, import, transform, and shape their data for business intelligence. Additionally, the Power BI course teaches you how to create dashboards and share them with business users on mobile devices and the web.

Managing your access on Azure's Active Directory

Azure Active Directory (AD) is a broad access and identity management solution. It provides a wide set of facilities, which allow you to supervise access to cloud and on-premises resources and applications. This includes various Microsoft online services, such as Office 365, in addition to numerous non-Microsoft SaaS applications.

One of the main features of Azure AD is that you can handle access to its resources. These resources can be external to the directory, like Software as a Service (SaaS) applications, on-premises resources or SharePoint sites, and Azure services, or they can be internal to the directory, such as permissions for managing objects through directory roles.

Chapter **11**

Getting Busy on IBM Bluemix

I n this chapter, I introduce you to IBM's blockchain initiatives, which IBM is merging with its other groundbreaking technologies, such as Bluemix, a full Platform as a Service (PaaS) for application building, and Watson, its super computer.

Blockchain technology creates a near-frictionless value exchange. Artificial intelligence accelerates the analysis of massive amounts of data. The merging of the two capabilities will be a paradigm shift that affects the way we do business and secure our connected electronic devices.

If you're involved in the Internet of Things (IoT), healthcare, warehousing, transportation, or logistics industries, you will benefit from the information in this chapter. Also, if you're an entrepreneur and would like to learn about the new capabilities that come with the integration of artificial intelligence (AI) and blockchain on a scalable app platform, this chapter is for you.

Business Blockchain on Bluemix

IBM is now offering blockchain technology that integrates with its traditional offerings, such as IBM Bluemix. Bluemix is an open-standards, cloud-based PaaS for building and managing applications. IBM has integrated a blockchain stack from Hyperledger, which is part of the Lynx foundation and is establishing best practices in blockchain technology.

You'll want to prepare for rapid and fundamental changes within IBM's blockchain initiatives. The technology is very new and still under incubation, both within IBM and Hyperledger.

Hyperledger has several different subprojects in development. As of this writing, IBM is using Fabric, but it may open up Bluemix to other projects. Fabric is open source and under active development within Hyperledger. You can start testing Fabric on Bluemix by using Hyperledger Fabric v0.6. However, IBM warns against running any valuable transactions directly on Fabric v0.6 or any earlier version.

Your isolated environment

Bluemix is the newest cloud offering from IBM. It's an implementation of IBM's open cloud architecture based on Cloud Foundry, an open-source PaaS.

Bluemix enables you to rapidly and easily come up with applications, deploy them, and manage them. Bluemix offers enterprise-level services that can integrate with applications without needing to know how to install or to configure them.

Figure 11-1 shows how IBM relates different aspects of blockchain and IBM systems. You can find out more at `https://goo.gl/12Q6no`.

IBM Bluemix provides four core things:

>> Computing infrastructure based on your apps' architectural needs

>> The ability to deploy apps to a Bluemix public or dedicated cloud

>> Dev tooling, such as code editors and managers

>> Access to third-party open-source tools in their service section

Bluemix gives you everything you need to build your app. It's now offering blockchain infrastructure to test as well.

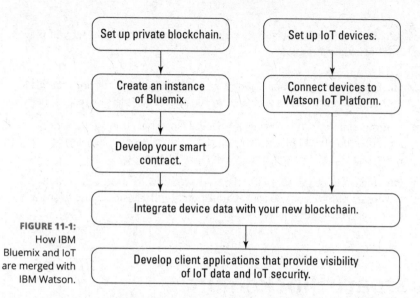

FIGURE 11-1:
How IBM
Bluemix and IoT
are merged with
IBM Watson.

They have a service for integrating your applications with the Bluemix blockchain. As of this writing, there are two pricing models. A free account gets you what you need to test your idea. You get four peers and a cert authority to sign transactions, as well as a dashboard with logs, controls, and APIs.

The enterprise plan is priced at $10,000 a month and offers higher security and speed than the free model.

Bluemix use cases

Two remarkable entrepreneurial pioneers are using Bluemix and the Hyperledger Fabric integration:

» **Wanxiang:** The largest China-based automotive components company, Wanxiang is working with IBM to deploy a private blockchain. They're embedding property rights into things like electric cars. The goal is to reduce the costs to consumers for leasing equipment. Wanxiang will use its blockchain technology to track the lifespan of the components and refurbish used batteries. Bluemix will take care of everything else.

» **KYCK!:** The financial technology (fintech) startup KYCK! is utilizing IBM's blockchain integration as a novel way to address "know your customer" (KYC) needs for brokerages. This expense is limiting and costly for banks and other financial services. KYC is done to prevent money laundering and illicit trade, and to combat terrorism. KYCK! is building a video conference and encrypted document submissions platform. It will allow brokers to work with and authenticate clients the company has not met in person.

IBM has also built out three simple Chaincode applications that let you play with the IBM Blockchain network:

>> **Marbles:** Marbles is an application that demonstrates transferring marbles between two users. It lets you see how you can move assets on a blockchain.

>> **Commercial Paper:** Commercial Paper is a blockchain trading network implemented on IBM Blockchain. You can create new commercial papers to trade, buy and sell existing trades, and audit the network.

>> **Car Lease:** Car Lease is a lot like the Marbles demo. It's designed to allow you to interact with assets. You can create, update, and transfer. It also allows a third party to view the history.

Watson's Smart Blockchain

IBM's supercomputer, Watson, is also available on the Bluemix platform. Watson is a cognitive computing artificially intelligent computer system. It can analyze structured and, more impressively, unstructured data at incredible speed.

WARNING

This technology is still developing, and customers have complained about its true ability to understand unstructured written language.

Watson can answer questions posed to it through natural language and learn as it absorbs more information. The implication of this technology, when married with blockchain technology, is astounding. One of the first implementations is within the IoT space. There is a strong need to secure data that is emitted from these devices and then make it actionable and intelligent.

Watson's Cognitive computing is simulating human thought processes and using the MQTT protocol. Like a human mind, it grows over time. Its self-learning systems use data mining, pattern recognition, and natural language processing to mimic the way your brain works. Watson processes at a rate of 80 teraflops per second (one teraflop is a trillion floating-point operations). To put this into context, that replicates — and in some cases surpasses — a high-functioning human's ability to answer questions. Watson is able to do this by accessing 90 servers with a combined data store of more than 200 million pages of information, which it processes against six million logic rules. Watson is about the size of ten refrigerators, but it's been getting smaller and faster.

Figure 11-2 shows the how IBM Watson relates different aspects of blockchain and IBM systems. Dive deeper at IBM https://goo.gl/12Q6no.

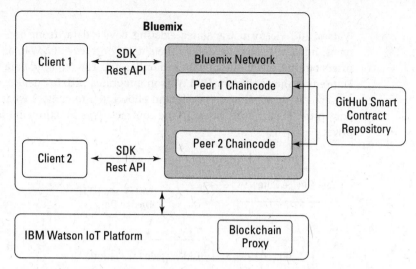

FIGURE 11-2:
How Bluemix
integrates clients,
peers, and IBM
Watson.

IBM is applying these amazing capabilities to IoT data feeds that utilize Chaincode implementation. Chaincode is a Hyperledger smart contract system. Here's how Watson-enabled blockchain for IoT devices will work:

>> IoT devices send data to your private blockchain ledgers for inclusion in shared transactions as a tamper-resistant record marked in time.

>> Partners and third-party service providers can access and supply IoT data as well, without the need for central control and management.

>> All parties can sign and verify data, limiting disputes and ensuring each partner is held accountable for their individual performances.

This is a simple implementation that does not take advantage of all the functionality and capabilities of Watson. Watson's ability to learn and make suggestions, and update out-of-date information will truly make it a powerful blockchain-enabled application in the future.

You can integrate Watson's IoT Platform with Fabric from Hyperledger. This integration allows you to execute Chaincode contracts through cognitive computing oracles. Watson's IoT platform has built-in capability that lets you add selected IoT data to your own private blockchain to create an oracle. This helps you protect the data from being viewed by unauthorized third parties.

When you've established a Bluemix workspace, you can add selective services, including the IoT Platform that integrates several technologies. Fabric is the blockchain technology that provides the private blockchain infrastructure for distributed peers that replicates the device data and validates the transaction through secure contracts.

Watson IoT Platform translates existing device data, from one or more device types, into the format needed by the smart contract APIs. Watson's IoT Platform filters out irrelevant device data and only sends the required data to the contract. Figure 11-3 shows the how IBM Watson integrates with IoT devices and APIs. Watson acts as the Chaincode oracle and allows you to control what information is known to the parties involved in the contract. This functionality is important for privacy.

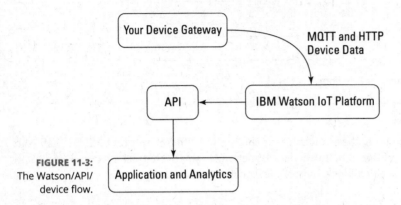

FIGURE 11-3:
The Watson/API/
device flow.

Building Your Starter Network on Big Blue

IBM's blockchain technology and IoT Platform offer new promising tools and can be leveraged to address many problems facing companies that are trying to scale:

>> **Security:** The huge volume of data that's collected from millions of devices raises information privacy concerns. Also, hacked IoT devices have been used by nefarious organizations to cripple websites with distributed denial of service attacks.

>> **Cost:** The high volume of messages, data generated by the devices, and analytical processes are going up as more devices come online and utilize that data.

>> **Architecture:** Centralized cloud platforms remain a bottleneck in end-to-end IoT solutions and a central point of attack.

IBM's open-standards-based distributed IoT networks can solve many of the problems associated with today's centralized, cloud-based IoT solutions. Connected devices communicate directly with distributed ledgers. Data from those devices is then be used by third parties to execute smart contracts, reducing the need for human monitoring.

The IBM Watson IoT Platform with a Fabric integration replicates data across a private blockchain network and eliminates the need to have all IoT data collected and stored centrally. Decentralized blockchain networks also improve the security of IoT devices. Unique digital identities are built for each device over time. This new way of creating and securing identity is exceptionally hard to spoof.

These new blockchain identities allow IoT devices to sign transactions that allow smart contracts to execute. A practical application of this would be an insurance product that was fed data from a smart car on the driving behavior of different individuals. The car would send data to be published in Fabric; the insurance product built with Chaincode would then recognize the new data and the identity of your car and update your policy.

The possibilities are nearly endless, and IoT has introduced huge opportunities for businesses and consumers, especially in the areas of healthcare, warehousing, transportation, and logistics.

There are three main tiers of IBM cloud–supported IoT solutions that meet the needs of different IoT business problems:

>> **Devices Gateway:** Device Gateway is for smart devices or sensors that collect data about the physical world. This could be things like weather sensors, temperature monitoring for refrigerated containers, or vital statistics data for a patient. These IoT devices send their data through the Internet for analysis and processing.

>> **IBM Watson IoT Platform:** IBM combines its supercomputer with its IoT Platform to collect data from IoT devices and then analyze the data and take subsequent actions to solve problems. Watson provides machine learning, machine reasoning, natural language processing, and image analysis that enhance the ability to process the unstructured data collected from the sensors.

>> **IBM Bluemix:** Bluemix is an open-standards-based cloud platform for building, running, and managing applications and services. It supports IoT applications by making it easy to include analytical and cognitive capabilities in those applications.

You can learn more about the IBM solution at https://developer.ibm.com/technologies/blockchain.

4

Industry Impacts

Understand the future of the financial services industry when it utilizes blockchain technology to move money around the world quickly and inexpensively.

Clarify your knowledge of global real estate as it relates to blockchain technology.

Identify opportunities in the insurance industry to reduce fraud and increase profits through new insurance instruments.

Examine the large-industry implications of permanent systems within government organizations and legal frameworks.

Clarify other large global trends in blockchain technology and how they'll shape the world you live in and the everyday tools you use.

Chapter **12**

Financial Technology

The first to adopt blockchain technology were banks, governments, and other financial institutions — and they're the fasting-growing blockchain users, too. The powerful tools that are being built to manage and move money will reshape our world in new and unexpected ways, so it makes sense that financial technology (fintech) would jump onboard.

This chapter gives you the inside scoop on what governments are currently doing with blockchain technology and how it will affect you. Fintech touches your life every day, whether you're aware of it or not.

In this chapter, I introduce you to future banking trends, new regulations, and the new tools that can help you move money faster and cheaper. I also explain new types of investment vehicles and other blockchain innovations. Finally, I warn you about potential risks of investments involving virtual currency and new blockchain-technology-enabled financial products.

Hauling Out Your Crystal Ball: Future Banking Trends

Banking was the first industry to recognize the threat of Bitcoin and then the potential of blockchain to transform the industry. The banking sector is highly regulated, and the fees to organize and operate as a bank are expensive.

These heavy regulations have been an insulating and protective shield for the whole industry, as well as a burden. The application of fast, efficient, digital money that doesn't carry the cost of handling cash and that is traceable as it moves through the financial system was an intoxicating and threatening proposal. The idea that value can be held outside the control of central authorities also piqued the interest of financial institutions and governments that back currencies.

Initially, these financial institutions and governments tried to squelch blockchain with regulation. Today, they're embracing blockchain through investment across the board.

In 2013 and 2014, the U.S. Securities and Exchange Commission (SEC) issued a warning to investors about the potential risks of investments involving virtual currency. The warning was that investors might be enticed with the promise of high returns and would not be skeptical enough of the new investment space that was so novel and cutting-edge. According to the SEC, digital currency was one of the top ten threats to investors. Today, the SEC stands ready to engage with companies and investors as cryptocurrency gains traction within all industries.

Not even two years later, countries around the world — including the UK, Canada, Australia, Japan, and China — began investigating how they could create their own digital currencies, seizing cryptocurrency for themselves and put money on the blockchain. In 2018, Venezuela launched a cryptocurrency called the Petro. The launch of the Petro is a significant turning point for cryptocurrency because Venezuela was the first sovereign nation to issue its own cryptocurrency.

Blockchain's promise of an uncompromisable ledger has been an appealing system to try for governments that are seeking to reduce fraud and improve trust. Innovations in blockchain technology promised to be able to handle the billions of transaction need to support economies, making a cryptocurrency feasible at scale.

Blockchains are in themselves permanent and unalterable records of every transaction that is inputted into it. Putting a country's money supply on a blockchain controlled by a central bank would be utterly transformative because there would be a permanent record of every financial transaction, existing at some level within their blockchain record, even if they weren't viewable to the public. Blockchain technology and digital currencies would reduce risk and fraud and give them ultimate control in executing monetary policy and taxation. It would not be anonymous like Bitcoin was at first. In fact, quite the opposite: It would allow them a full and auditable trail of every digital transaction made by individuals and companies. It might even allow central banks to replace commercial banks' role in circulating money.

The question of what the future for banking will look like can be scary and exciting. Consumers can now pay friends through their phones almost instantly in almost any type of currency or cryptocurrency. More and more retail stores have begun utilizing cryptocurrency as a way to pay for goods and accept payment from customers. In Kenya, using cryptocurrency is more normal than not. But this is still not the mainstream option for most of the world. Western markets are still in the early adoption phase.

Given that most individuals have their wealth locked into legal tender issued by governments or locked into assets that are within existing government systems, fintech innovations must merge with these existing systems before we see the mainstream utility of blockchain or digital currencies. If regulators find ways to tax and register accounts, mass adoption of customer-facing wallets with digitized tokens is two or three years down the road.

The business-to-business market will start utilizing blockchain much quicker. A production-hardened system with the associated policies and operations is being tested. Ripple and R3 among others have been hard at work making this possible. These systems will first focus on the institutional creation of digitized representations of deposits. These are IOUs between internal organizational departments and between trusted partners, like vendors. Regulators, central banks, and monetary authorities are all investing heavily in making this possible. Canada and Singapore have been moving very quickly.

Know your customer (KYC) and anti-money-laundering (AML) regulations require banks to know who they're doing business with and ensure that they're not participating in money laundering or terrorism. Banks issuing cryptocurrencies still have significant challenges to overcome first. In order to stay compliant with KYC and AML regulations, they need to know the identity of all the individuals utilizing their currency. In many cases, people's bank accounts are already debit and credit service of transactions, like distributed ledgers in blockchains, except for centralized. The first candidates in this area are going to be regions where regulators, banks, and central banks work together. Singapore and Dubai are good candidates that already have blockchain initiatives.

Moving money faster: Across borders and more

Assessing the transaction volume needed to be met by a blockchain handling the currency of an economy like the UK or U.S. is difficult. The U.S. alone is processing billions of transactions a day and over $17 trillion in value a year. That's a lot of responsibility for a new technology! The nation would be crippled if its monetary supply were compromised.

The International Monetary Fund, the World Bank, the Bank for International Settlements, and central bankers from all over the world have met to discuss blockchain technology. The first step toward faster and cheaper money would be adopting a blockchain as the protocol to facilitate bank transfers and interbank settlement. Official digital currencies that ordinary citizens use on a daily basis would come much later.

Individual consumers wouldn't directly feel the cost reduction from utilizing a blockchain for interbank settlement. The savings would be seen in the bank's bottom line as cost reductions for fees charged by intermediaries.

Consumers will still want retail locations and commercial banks for the foreseeable future. But millennials have already adopted app-activated payments through PayPal, Venmo, Cash, and more. A new way of paying through their phones won't faze them.

The great challenge is that if all money is digital, compromising it could be catastrophic. It's possible that the architecture of blockchain systems could be strong enough. The issue might be instead that the code within the system is executed in an unexpected manner, as happened in the decentralized autonomous organization (DAO) hack on Ethereum (see Chapter 5). If the cryptocurrency were operating on a traditional public blockchain, then 51 percent of the nodes in the network would have to agree to fix the issue. Getting an agreement in place might take a lot of time, and it wouldn't be practical for businesses and people who need stable and secure money at all times.

Many blockchains operate as democracies. A majority (51 percent) of a blockchain's nodes network are needed to make a change.

Creating permanent history

Data sovereignty and digital privacy are going to be huge topics in the future. Fraud prevention will be easier because if the whole economy is utilizing a cryptocurrency, there will always be an auditable trail inside the blockchain that secures it. This is enticing for law enforcement, but a nightmare for consumer privacy.

From a customer perspective, there's already an audit trail for everything you purchase with a credit or debit card. From an institution perspective, it's a beneficial to have audit trails because it increases transparency of documentation and life cycles of the movements of these assets between different regions. It adds legitimacy to the trading of assets and allows them to bake compliance into their day-to-day transactions.

The "right to be forgotten" rules in Europe, which allow citizens the right to not have their data forever propagated on the Internet, are a difficult challenge for blockchains, because blockchains can never forget. Governments and corporations would have permanent historical records of every transaction, which could be devastating to national security if they were exposed to the public. Or in a company's case, it may allow their competitors to have an inside scoop on how their competitors are investing.

The biggest challenge to using a permissionless blockchain such as Ethereum or Bitcoin would be guaranteeing that you haven't sent money to an OFAC country to support terrorism. The answer is that you can't because there are somewhat anonymous and anyone can open a wallet. It is possible to create algorithms to trace transaction movement — the U.S. government has been doing this for years — but anyone can move value in a permissionless world.

The Office of Foreign Asset Control maintains sanctions on specific organizations or individuals in what are considered high-threat countries. The government is unable to track the history of transactions when using permissionless platforms anonymously.

The need for KYC and AML makes a case for the permissioned blockchain in the shared ledger space. The software company R3 developed Corda, a private and permissioned blockchain-like platform to meet many of these challenges directly. They specifically do not globally broadcast the data from their participants. This keeps the data within the Corda blockchain private and was the primary nonfunctional requirement requested by the more than 75 banks that worked with R3 to adopt blockchain technology. They need to maintain their privacy and meet strong regulatory demands.

Going International: Global Financial Products

Blockchains will usher in many new types of securities and investment products. New markets will be opening with more efficient ways of calculating risk because collateral will be a lot more transparent and fungible across institutions when they accounted for it within a blockchain back system.

Blockchain technology also has applications in helping reduce scams within the global warehouse market for fraudulent double-sold goods. Blockchain entries enable manufacturers and regulators to document the provenance of products and, in turn, allows buyers to check the authenticity of what they're buying. There are several solutions in the market, including Everledger and Provenance.

TIP

Hernando de Soto, the famous Peruvian economist, estimates that by providing the world's poor with titles for their land, homes and unregistered businesses would unlock $9.3 trillion in assets. This is what is meant by the term *dead capital*.

It is imaginable that countries that can free their dead capital, the unfinanceable real property they own, they will be able to bundle and sell these interest in these assets across a global marketplace. This would be things like transparent mortgage-backed securities for new real estate developments in Colombia or Peru.

In the future, countries will be able to free up their dead capital. Owners of properties, undeveloped land, and un-financeable properties will now have the opportunity to sell the interests in these assets across a global marketplace.

These assets will be appealing because asset managers will be able to actively parse underperforming assets given the transparency and capability of one being substituted in place of another through blockchain-based technology. The use of blockchains to manage these assets will give managers the power always to own top-performing securities, removing the rotten apples, reclassifying them, and selling them as new securities.

For non-institutional customers, micro-investments will be an attractive outlet enabled globally and locally through blockchain trading platforms. Using blockchain technology will also give them the means of investing in companies and their specific activities without having minimums or going through intermediaries that take a percentage of the investment.

Decentralized autonomous organizations (DAOs) are already out there and making DAO investment pools happen for a few risk-tolerant and more technically savvy investors. It may be some time before an institutional investor utilizes one or a portfolio manager recommends putting money into a DAO-based vehicle for her clients.

DAOs remove a lot of the necessary paperwork and bureaucracy involved in investing by creating a blockchain-based voting system and giving shares to those who invest in their product. To any blockchain, the "code as law" concept makes it unforgiving. The risks are many, particularly when there is poorly written code that executes in unintended ways. The consequences are that hacks to this system can be severe. The transparent nature of the original system, the poor code, gives hackers a wider attack vector and allows them to attack multiple times as they gain more and more information each time.

In the following section, I discuss the effects and benefits of blockchain technology on the world economy.

Border-free payroll

Our world is global, and companies don't have borders. Instant and nearly free payroll is enticing and would save a lot of headaches for organizations. But there are drawbacks, too.

The largest risks will be with the loss of funds through hacking. If you're compensated in cryptocurrency, and you were hacked, it would be impossible to retrieve your funds. There's no dispute resolution center. There's no customer service to complain to for the loss of these funds. Thieves of digital currency have global access while being somewhat anonymous. The hacker could be anywhere.

With the current structure of blockchains, the consumer is responsible for his own security. Currently, customers don't have the main burden of protecting and insuring themselves from a loss. Larger companies and governments offer protection and insurance, and they have for as long as anyone can remember. Regular individuals haven't had to protect themselves in this manner since they stopped holding their own gold during medieval times (more or less).

These challenges haven't spotted companies from processing payroll using cryptocurrency. Bitwage and BitPay are both competing in the market for payroll processing via Bitcoin. Bitwage allows employees and independent contractors to receive part of their paychecks in cryptocurrency, even if their employers don't offer the option. BitPay, on the other hand, has payroll service providers Zuman and Incoin integrated into its payment and payroll APIs. Again, early adoption is happening in areas that had nonexistent or inadequate solutions before.

Faster and better trade

Blockchains will facilitate faster and possible more inclusive trade. Global trade finance has restricted in recent years. Some banks like Barclays have even pulled out of growing African markets. They leave behind a vacuum for financing trade. Companies still need capital to ship their goods.

DAOs and micro investments could meet that need and give investors more profitable returns than are currently available on the market. Transparency of all the goods being sold, secure identity, and seamless global tracking that is all connected to a blockchain would open up this opportunity for small investors.

The interoperability between currencies, which companies like Ripple facilitate, will also allow for more trade because they offer flexible ways of calculating foreign exchange rates than through the transfer mechanisms. The introduction of more popular digital currencies into foreign currency exchanges will add to the adaptability and integration of underserved markets.

BitPesa is a company that converts M-pesa phone minutes from Kenya into Bitcoin. With this technology, it offers businesses a faster and cheaper way to send or receive payments between Africa and China. The trade between Africa and China is a market of over $170 billion. It takes days to settle payments across borders, and the fees are high. When you use BitPesa's digital platform, payments are instantaneous and cheap.

Guaranteed payments

Guaranteed payments that are permitted through blockchain-backed transactions will increase trade in places where trust is low. Poorer countries can compete on the same playing field as wealthier nations within these types of systems. As this happens over the next ten years, the global economies will shift. The cost of commodities and labor may increase.

Global companies pay their employees based on competitive pricing, as well as on employees' previous salaries. If blockchains allow for equality across economic divides, it won't happen overnight. Developers and other knowledge workers would be the exception because it'll be easier for them to support themselves based on anonymous work.

Financial inclusion and equal global trade are very important topics for governments. Adoption of digital currencies will more likely be done nationwide in small and developing countries. Most large countries have decentralized power structures that prevent quick changes to vital systems like money.

Their central power structures of small countries will allow them to leapfrog over legacy infrastructure and bureaucracy. For example, most African and South American countries don't have landlines or addresses, but they all have smartphones and ability to create cryptocurrency wallets. The missing piece is overall trade liquidity and capacity to pay for basic needs such as utilities, rent, and food through a cryptocurrency.

Micropayments: The new nature of transactions

Micropayments are the new form of transactions. Credit card companies may use blockchain technology to settle the transaction, reduce fraud, and lower their own costs.

Global institutions like Visa and MasterCard, which provide the benefit of delayed payment, will always be needed by consumers in capitalistic societies. Even if the backend changes, you still have the same access points for customers. But physical cards will go away. In fact, that's happening now, even without blockchain technology. With blockchain technology, the customer identities behind payments will be more hardened against theft.

People still need credit to operate a business and get by personally. Credit card companies will keep making money through transaction fees. Credits run the world, and capital markets will always exist in our current social structure. The cost of sending money between groups will decrease, but that's a good thing for financial institutions. They want to focus on the service of providing their customers with the best choices in their investment or banking markets.

Squeezing Out Fraud

Bitcoin was created as an answer to the financial crisis, where fraud and other unethical actions caused the world economy to collapse. It shifts from a "trust or doesn't trust" view of the world to a trustless system. This subtle difference is lost to most. A *trustless system* is one in which you equally trust and mistrust every person within the network. More important, the blockchain provides a framework that allows transactions to occur without trust.

These same types of frameworks can be used in more than just exchanging value over the network. Let me share an example that will help illustrate the potential.

I go to a bar and the man at the door stops me and asks to see my ID. I reach into my wallet and hand him my driver's license. My license has a lot of information on it that the bouncer doesn't need, nor should he have access to (like my address). All he needs from the ID is that I'm over the age of 21. He doesn't even need to know how old I am — just that I meet the regulation requirements.

In the future, blockchain ID systems will let you choose what information you expose to what person and at what level. The more anonymous data it has, the safer it will be. Blockchain systems will help curb the theft of identity and data by not sharing information with those who don't need it or have permission to see it.

Another aspect of blockchain technology is that it will shift fraud from where it happened (past tense) to where it is currently happening in real time. Within our current system, audits are fractional post-mortems of what has happened. A group of outside auditors comes, pulls a few random files, and sees if everything is in place. Doing anything beyond this is too costly and time-consuming.

Record systems that have blockchain technology integrated within them will be able to audit a file as it's created, flagging incomplete or unusual files as they're created. This will give managers the tools they need to proactively correct files before they become a problem.

Another feature of blockchain systems will be the ability to share the data with third parties transparently. In the future, sharing data will be as easy as emailing a zip file, except the receiver will then have access to the original copy, not a copy if the file sent across email. When someone sends a file, he has a version on his computer and the receiver has a version. With blockchain technology, the two people will only be sharing one version.

Blockchains act as a third party that witnesses the age and creation of files. They can tell at a granular level each person who interacted with a file across systems, internally and externally. They can show what is missing from a file, not just the data that is contained in it now. Blockchain files can also be shared in a redacted fashion that does not compromise the validity of documents.

What this means is that you'll be able to see the age of a file, the complete history of a file, and what it looked like over time as it evolved. More interestingly, you'll also be able to see if anything is missing from a file. This concept is called *proving the negative.* Most file systems at this point can only tell you what they have within them. But you'll be able to tell what a file *doesn't* have.

Auditing will be less expensive and more complete. Updating audit rules could be done in a more centralized way. When regulatory nodes within a blockchain network have a shared and transparent view into asset transactions, the reporting of these transactions can be done through the regulator's location, without mandating 100 or more other institutions to adhere to the same rule set.

Blockchain-based systems that are fully integrated across an organization will be able to know where every penny was spent. The last mile of how money is spent is the most difficult to account for across organizations and governments. Because it's so difficult to account for, those wishing to steal funds have the opening they need.

The last mile could become a company's greatest opportunity to save wasted resources and identify corrupt individuals. Nonprofits that have strict guidelines on accounting for how they spend their money could benefit from this type of system the most. They could meet their needs for auditing and accountability to their donors without impeding them in their greater missions for good.

One system that has been explored would integrate directly into the workflow of aid workers. This system was originally designed to track medical records but could also track back all the supplies that are used with each medical patient. The benefits of this system would be monumental, given that so much fraud and theft occurs within the NGO world.

Chapter **13**

Real Estate

Real estate will be one of the industries most impacted by innovations in blockchain technology. The impact will be felt in every country in a slightly different way. In the western world, we might see the advent of things like transparent mortgage-backed securities traded on blockchain-enabled exchanges. In China, blockchain integration is already happening with things like notarization, an essential component of real estate transactions. In the developing world, blockchains hold the most promise because they may be able to free capital and increase trade.

This chapter dives into the innovations that are already happening around the world in the real estate industry. I also fill you in on possible changes coming down the road and the significant implications of blockchain technology.

Real estate holds much of the world's wealth and economic stability. The industry will be changing very quickly over the next few years, and knowing where these changes will occur and how you and your company can take advantage of them will be a benefit.

Eliminating Title Insurance

Title insurance is compensation for financial loss from defects in your title for a real estate purchase. It's required if you take out a mortgage on your home or if you refinance it. Title insurance protects the bank's investment against title problems that might not be found in the public records, are missed in the title search, or occur from fraud or forgery.

Title insurance is necessary in places that use common law to govern their title systems. The buyer is responsible for ensuring that the seller's title is good. Within these systems, a title search is done and insurance is bought. In areas that use a Torrens title system a buyer can rely on the information in the land register and doesn't need to look beyond those records.

Blockchain technology has been proposed as a supplement to help consumers in common law title systems. The idea is simple: Blockchains are fantastic public recordkeeping systems; they also can't be backdated or changed without a record. In theory, blockchains could transform common law systems into distributed Torrens title systems.

First, though, many challenges must be overcome. Each county in a common law system has its own land records office, where all the deeds or records that transfer title to any piece of land or any interest in any land in the county are recorded and noted. The United States alone has thousands of counties. The thousands of individual offices create silos of data. Blockchain doesn't change the law or how the records are organized.

New laws would need to be created that dictate that all interest and transfer of land must be recorded within a single system to be valid. Then it's just a Torrens system and may make blockchain technology redundant. The exception would be in areas where there is a lot of fraud within the land registry.

In the following sections, I dig into the real estate industry and where blockchains add value.

Protected industries

Every industry has self-protecting systems to keep new competition out. It might be a high regulatory burden, government-granted monopolies, or high startup costs. The industry that has built up around the buying and selling of real estate hasn't changed much in the last 40 years and is ripe for disruption. Many different parties contribute to the process.

Here are the different industries that are built around the buying and selling of homes:

>> **Real estate agents:** A real estate agent helps you compare different neighborhoods and find a home. He often helps you negotiate a price and communicates with the seller on your behalf. This service is valuable, and it's not likely to be displaced by blockchain technology. You can already buy a home without a real estate agent — people choose to work with them because they improve the process.

>> **Home inspectors:** Home inspectors uncover defects with the house before you buy it — defects that could cost you money down the road. The defects home inspectors find can be used to negotiate with the seller for a better price. In the future, homes will continue to have wear and tear — that'll never change. But blockchain technology could be used to record repairs to property and defects found in the inspection.

>> **Closing representatives:** At closing, the final step is settlement. The closing representative supervises and coordinates the closing documents, records them, and releases the money to the appropriate parties. Closing representatives may be displaced by blockchain technology — the functions performed by closing representatives could be built into smart contracts or chaincode.

>> **Mortgage lenders and servicers:** Mortgage lenders and servicers provide funds for a mortgage and collect the ongoing mortgage payments. They won't be displaced with blockchain software, but they may use blockchain technology to help them reduce costs with recordkeeping and auditing.

>> **Real estate appraisers:** The real estate appraiser's job is to look at a property and determine how much it's worth. The appraisal process is done every time a property is bought or refinanced. Companies like Zillow have taken a lot of the legwork out of knowing the market value, but each home is unique and needs to be assessed periodically. Even in the real estate mortgage process, multiple appeals may be called for to meet everyone's needs. It might be useful to record this data within a blockchain as a public witness.

>> **Loan officers:** Loan officers use your credit, financial, and employment information to see if you qualify for a mortgage. They then match what you're eligible for with products that they sell. Like a real estate agent, a loan officer helps you get the best option across a spectrum of choices. Blockchain software may be used to help loan officers keep track of documents that they give you and audit the process for fair lending law compliance.

>> **Loan processors:** A loan processor assists loan officers in preparing mortgage loan information and the application for presentation to the underwriter. Software that pulls the buyer's source information is being explored. It's not blockchain technology, but it could be disruptive for this position.

>> **Mortgage underwriters:** A mortgage underwriter determines whether you're eligible for a mortgage loan. She approves or rejects your mortgage loan application based on your credit history, employment, assets, and debts. Organizations are exploring automating the underwriting process using artificial intelligence. It's not blockchain technology, though.

Each of these agents serves a core purpose that helps protect the buyer, seller, and mortgage provider. In most industries, the cost of doing business goes down over time — improvements in efficiency brought about by competition and innovation contribute to driving down cost. The mortgage industry is attractive as a candidate for blockchain innovation, because the opposite has occurred: The cost of business has gone up. The typical U.S. mortgage is over 500 pages and costs $7,500 to originate. This is three times what it cost ten years ago. Blockchain technology can meet the needs of protecting the buyer, seller, and mortgage provider while reducing the cost to do so.

Consumers and Fannie Mae

The Federal National Mortgage Association (known as Fannie Mae) is both a government-sponsored enterprise and a publicly traded company. It's currently the leading source of financing for mortgage lenders and has dominated the market post-recession as private money left.

Since the recession, 95 percent of all home loans made in the United States have come through Fannie Mae. This is about $5 trillion in mortgage assets. With few exceptions, loans that are not done through Fannie Mae or its close cousin, Freddie Mac, are jumbo loans (typically more than $417,000 each). These loans are still funded through private money.

Fannie Mae has an automated program used by loan originators to qualify a borrower. It helps them navigate guidelines for a conventional loan. Lenders run your loan application through Fannie Mae's computer system, and it spits out an answer of either approve or decline for your loan. Online platforms are using this new software to reach consumers, allowing them to bypass traditional retail locations. Fannie Mae and Freddie Mac are exploring blockchain technology to even further streamline this process and reach customers directly.

Mortgages in the Blockchain World

A mortgage in a blockchain world won't seem that much different than a mortgage in the traditional world. The part that you'll notice is that a blockchain mortgage will be less expensive at closing.

Given that most people only ever buy a few homes in their lifetimes, the difference may not seem like a big deal. But the money does add up. Blockchain technology could lower the cost to originate a mortgage back to pre-2007 levels.

Reducing your origination costs

Mortgage origination costs have increased, and the reason is simple: Banks fear fines that they can incur if they mess up any part of the mortgage process. So, the industry has put in steps to help make sure that they meet all the requirements at the time of origination and years later when they're audited. Big banks have paid billions in fines from the mishandling of documents. They're now required not only to have all the essential documents, but also to prove that they followed the correct process and sent you all the necessary documents.

Blockchain-based products reduce the redundancy that banks began incorporating into their process after the recession. Recordkeeping and auditing expenses have skyrocketed since the introduction of the Dodd–Frank Wall Street Reform and Consumer Protection Act, and blockchain technology could reduce that cost.

Companies wanting to meet the needs of banks with a blockchain solution would need to let banks prove that they followed the guidelines set out in Dodd–Frank. It would also help banks document why they made certain decisions on loans, and help them locate documents that were used in origination, even if they aren't in possession of them.

Blockchain applications could put close to $4,000 back on the table for the average home purchase. The mortgage industry is a lot like the car loan industry and the credit card industry. Similar applications could reduce the administration cost that these industries have due to consumer protection laws, while at the same time letting companies meet those requirements.

Knowing your last-known document

One of the largest cost drivers in the mortgage origination process often comes years after the loan was first made. Sometimes those facilitating the loan process add unneeded documents into client files, or old files that aren't used to originate a loan are left in the folder. Also, duplicate records may occur. When it comes time to audit the file, there is too much information to sift through. Banks pay money to outside firms to check their records and try to determine what documents were used in the final dissection on your loan.

Blockchain software can solve this problem in an elegant way. Blockchains are distributed recordkeeping systems that allow for multiple parties to collaborate on data over time without losing track of what that data looked like at any given point along the way. This means that the half dozen individual organizations that collaborate to help you buy your home can now all interact on the same chain.

A chain in this use case would start with you. Your chain would then have sub-chains added to it over time, such as the purchase of a home. You could then authorize others — such as banks, employers, credit agencies, appraisal companies, and the like — to write against the chain. They would each add their data to your chain, and the other authorized parties could read this data and add their own.

Blockchains would change the need for central repositories for files. It would automate some of the processing of the paperwork, and would always give a clear history of your loan, reducing the need to audit and prepare documents to be verified.

This is a big idea, but it doesn't require the whole ecosystem to collaborate. Each branch that does would strengthen the system and add value, much like the way each addition person who owned a fax machine made the power of having one that much more useful.

Forecasting Regional Trends

Blockchain has been fighting an uphill battle to become a mainstream software solution. It is often met with fear because many people don't understand how it works or what the actual implications are for its widespread implementation. Also, many of the early advocates, like early adopters of any new technology, were seen as a little "out there." Blockchain gets caught up in the bad PR of Bitcoin and illicit and illegal things being done with the technology.

However, 2016 was a turning point for the industry. It became clear that blockchain would be disruptive and that those who wanted to be on the positive side of that equation had to come up with a blockchain strategy.

Every major bank began programs to investigate and experiment with blockchain or joined a consortium. Many moved first to interbank settlement and cross-border transfers, which are relatively straightforward applications for blockchains. The next and more transformative evolutions will be the systems and data that are secured through decentralization.

In the following sections, I cover the trends in blockchain technology in the United States, Europe, China, and Africa.

The United States and Europe: Infrastructure congestion

The United States and European countries may take longer to implement block-chain technology than other countries. Even though companies in these countries spend billions of dollars on infrastructure maintenance, it's just that: mainte-nance. There are already existing solutions to the problems that blockchains want to solve. It's not just a matter of saying that blockchains would offer a better solution — that solution must be ten times better than an existing system or be able to implement through integration.

One of the main challenges that the United States faces is that it's decentralized in the distribution of power and decision-making. Each county and each state will come up with its own rules for how to implement or use blockchain technology. This process has already begun.

Blockchains can trigger money transmitter laws and regulations. In the United States, it's clearer at a federal level what types of businesses are considered money transmitters. Given that all the essential public blockchains currently use a cryp-tocurrency token to drive security, the issue is clouded, which has given rise to private and permission blockchains that operate without tokens.

State licensure requirements are ambiguous for companies using blockchain technology for applications other than payments. Regulations and laws will be enacted to protect consumers. Europe already has laws around "being forgotten." Compliance with these rules could be tricky when data entered into blockchains is around forever and can't be removed by anyone, even if they wanted to.

Being engaged in money transmission in many U.S. states is a felony if you aren't properly licensed. The hard consequences of overstepping law through innovation compel blockchain companies to spend significantly more money and time on compliance — to the tune of an average of $2 million to $7 million per year per company because they must meet regulatory requirements in all 50 states. The legal fees are heavy burdens for these technology startups.

The legislation of each state as applied to the blockchain industry are not clear yet. New York and Vermont have begun integrating this technology into law. New York has increased the cost to be in compliance and driven innovation to move to friendlier locations. Vermont, on the other hand, passed a law that makes block-chain records admissible in court.

Luxembourg created a legal framework for electronic payment establishments in 2011 and was early on the idea of "electronic money." Luxembourg and the UK have become home to many blockchain companies because the regulatory environment is easier for them to navigate and afford. For less than $1 million, blockchain businesses can obtain a payment instrument license in the European Union. This license grants companies access to 28 EU countries. This approach has allowed the EU to advance beyond the United States in fintech innovation.

China: First out of the gate

China realized that citizens were using it to move value out of the country undetected and were generating new wealth in a less captive system. Because of this, China has revised its regulations on cryptocurrency several times, which has had a significant impact on the market price of Bitcoins.

Industries inside of China are looking to blockchains to solve many of the same problems seen in other parts of the world. They've been quick to use blockchains to supplement what they've already been doing, adding layers of certainty to things like Internet of Things (IoT) and notarization. Whereas Western countries have a more distributed and decentralized power structure, China has a more centralized one. This allows China to move quickly to both regulate and innovate.

China Ledger, a blockchain coalition with support from the Chinese National Assembly, the ruling body of China, is a good example of swift action by both regulatory bodies and industry. China Ledger has attracted Anthony Di Iorio and Vitalik Buterin, both Ethereum founders. It also has support from Bitcoin core developer Jeff Garzik and UBS Innovation Manager Alex Baltin.

Another China-based project that has been leading the charge in blockchain technology is Distributed Credit Chain (DCC), which is building distributed-bank systems. The DCC network has created business operation standards, ledger consensus, business contract assignments, and clearing and settlement for financial service providers.

The developing world: Roadblocks to blockchain

The future is here — it's just not distributed. This is especially true in developing countries, which often have a greater need for technology, yet don't have the same resources or the right political environment to allow those innovations to take root. Some small countries try protectionist measures that block the importation of goods that could be made within their borders; other countries mistrust the quality and benevolence of products and services that come from the outsides sources as well. On a darker note, some political systems benefit too greatly from the inefficiencies and ambiguities that their legal system has in place to change.

Hernando de Soto Polar is a Peruvian economist and author who has spoken widely on an informal economy and the importance of business and property rights. One of the prominent issues that keeps the developing world undeveloped is *dead capital.* The property which is informally held and not legally recognized or the current systems in place cannot be trusted. For owners of this land, it is difficult or impossible to finance and sell. The uncertainty also decreases the value of the assets. The western world has been able to borrow against assets and sell them relatively freely. This has driven innovation and economic prosperity.

The technology that is enabled by blockchains could change that reality for developing countries very quickly. Clear ownership records for land would mean that it would be sellable and financeable. This would make the beachfront property of Colombia irresistible. Irreversible payments and true known identity would open credit and commerce in new ways.

Many startups and hackers have come together to try to make this future vision a reality. Even larger global players like the World Bank have had repeated meeting about blockchain and its impact in the developing world. Bitcoin and blockchain are making inroads in Africa where local currencies and infrastructure are deeply mistrusted. BitPesa, a payment and trading platform servicing many countries in Africa, has begun expanding to the UK and Europe. It has also started widening its service offerings to things like payroll.

As many roadblocks as developing countries have toward development and innovation, they also have advantages that western countries will never overcome. The lack of existing infrastructure in developing countries makes it easier for them to leapfrog Western nations. This was evident in the proliferation of cellphones in developing countries. Developing countries also don't have the same regulatory bodies and consumer protections. This is particularly attractive for blockchain startups that fall into the gray zone in western countries. Developing countries often have fewer decision makers, making it easier to meet people who have the power to change.

Chapter **14**

Insurance

Blockchain insurance technology is situated to change how individuals and companies buy and obtain insurance coverage, and it's being tested by companies you may know, like Toyota. You need to understand the implications of these new technologies that are just now on the horizon.

In this chapter, I explain how these new technologies work and their core limitations. I show you how Internet of Things (IoT) devices will collaborate with insurance providers. I also describe how self-executing blockchain contracts will shape policies and company structures.

This chapter prepares you for the fundamental changes in technology that may shift the burden of proof. After reading this chapter, you'll be able to make more educated decisions about blockchain-based insurance coverage and payments. You'll understand how the cost of coverage will affect you and the different types of coverage that will become available to you in the future.

Precisely Tailoring Coverage

IoT devices, immutable data, decentralized autonomous organizations (DAOs), and smart contracts are all shifting the development of insurance for consumers. The convergence of all these technologies is possible because of the development of blockchains.

Blockchains do a few things really well that will allow for two major shifts in how insurance will be bought and sold in the future: Individuals will be able to gain more custom coverage, and new markets will open up that weren't possible before due to costs.

Insuring the individual

Insurance built around the individual will allow for a significant shift of priorities. Asset management will be less critical, and the insurers will be able to focus on risk calculation and matching supply and demand.

You could create a marketplace platform that insures customers. There are many ways that you could organize this new business. One possibility would be an on-demand marketplace where users post their requests, either standardized by custom smart contract or by Chaincode contract. If you haven't read about these types of new self-executing digital contracts, check out Chapter 5 on Ethereum and Chapter 9 on Hyperledger.

With this type of model, you, as the insurer, could calculate the premium for the specific demand, based on historical data and other risk calculation factors in your risk model. If the customer is satisfied with the offer, the customer can bid or subscribe, depending on the demand model being utilized.

This new type of insurance could be adopted by peer-to-peer (P2P) or crowd-funded insurance or a traditional insurance company that adopts the technology. Either way, both are created in a decentralized cryptocurrency ledger with the use of smart contracts/Chaincode, which guarantee the payment from the customer to the investor and vice versa if an incident occurs. Blockchain is key here, because it enables a few things that weren't feasible or secure a few years ago.

Blockchains create near frictionless transfer of value meaning micropayments are feasible because the transaction fees are so low. You can now open up new markets that did not have a working monetary system or legal system or instances where the cost of transactions and disputes outweighed the benefit of offering coverage.

You can use DAOs, with smart contracts, to govern large groups at a fraction of the cost and time. You could use this model to incorporate and administer your new company, and possibly crowd-fund insurance platforms.

The self-executing nature of smart contracts could also illuminate many of the cost of claims adjustment and third parties that help with the processing and collection of funds.

The legality of all this is still in question. Determining privacy concerns and consumer rights is difficult. The country also has its own regulations and disclosures. However, when those regulations are met, the insurance industry and the consumer's experience with insurance will shift substantially.

The new world of micro insurance

Micro insurance is insurance to protect low-income people against risk, such as accident, illness, and natural disaster. It has become more feasible through blockchain technology.

When thinking about micro insurance, pay attention to two categories (which can go hand in hand):

>> Insurance targeted to low-income households, farmers, and other entities where the insurance is designed around specific needs — typically, a low-premium and index-based insurance

>> Insurance that deals with low-value products or services

The biggest issue with these types of contracts within traditional insurance models is that their handling costs are disproportionately high and make it unattractive to serve these markets.

The low-friction attribute of blockchains allows them to move value at extremely low cost, nearly instantly anywhere in the world, with no charge backs, opens up the opportunity of serving more people and at lower costs.

The key advantage of blockchain is that the creation of smart contracts allows for secure transactions without any middleman, so insurance has significantly lower costs.

The blockchain micro insurance principle is simple and consists of four steps:

1. Lending/insuring agreement proposal

   A person can offer to lend his property through his insurance provider, if the property is digitally registered. The offer can be sent to the potential user, either through the insurance company channels or via a public platform such as Facebook.

2. Agreement review

   The borrower can then review the proposal that he received and accept or decline it. The offer is kept in the public records, and if the borrower accepts the proposal, he can purchase the insurance through standard payment channels, and the process moves to the third step.

3. Agreement signature and notarization

   If both parties are on the same page, the insurance is paid for and the borrower receives the property in question, the agreement is digitally signed and notarized onto a blockchain. This makes it virtually tamper-proof. All the transaction information is safely stored with a clear audit trail if it's ever needed.

4. Confirmation tokens

   Both parties receive special digital tokens that serve as the proof of identity for the agreement in question. These tokens are used to cryptologically confirm that both parties have signed the agreement.

Besides this ease of use, smart contracts allow for index-based insurance, which is very useful for agricultural insurance and other fields where the values depend greatly on dynamic factors that can be accurately documented by trusted third parties. In this particular case, insured farmers can receive automated payouts when particular conditions, such as drought, are reported by verified meteorological databases, thus further reducing potential service cost.

Witnessing for You: The Internet of Things

Blockchains enable the creation of a new type of identity for both people and things. They build on a traditional model where a certificate authority issues a certificate. For people, that certificate would be a document such as a birth certificate or a driver's license. But "things" have similar certificates that help consumers validate quality and authenticity.

These types of certificates have been knocked off for years. More and more sophisticated security has gone into their creation, but this increases the cost. Blockchains allow for the recording of these traditional certificates in an unalterable history that anyone can look up and reference. An added feature is the ability to update those records as new events occur.

IoT devices can now publish all kinds of data autonomously to their records and update the current state they're in. Now that IoT devices can speak for themselves and have their histories and identities published and sharable with third parties, insurance will be just one of the many industries affected.

IoT projects in insurance

IoT will likely have significant impact in three areas of your life: the connected car, the connected home, and the connected self.

The IoT is, at its core, a disruptive technology and, as such, it'll change the shape of a broad range of industries, such as automotive original equipment manufacturers (OEMs), home security, and cable and mobile providers. In that mix are insurance companies — in particular, the ones that work with property and casualty (P&C) policies.

The data gathered by the sensors in the new appliances and devices, along with the automation and additional control options, will lead to new possibilities when it comes to new companies emerging in the insurance industry. Combined with the blockchain decentralized ledgers and smart contracts, the whole process could be automated to a level that would've been impossible before.

WARNING

The new, always online, lifestyle that comes with such a radical shift in technology removes some of the existing risks, but it introduces new ones, the most important of which is information security. All this means that the risk factors will have to be recalculated. For example, self-driving cars will have reduced risk of accident due to the absence of human error, but the reliability of the technology will be in question until we have enough data from real-world application.

Implications of actionable big data

Big data has been a thing since 2000, and nowadays it's a $200 billion industry and of particular importance to the financial sector. However, big data comes with a number of problems that only grow with its presence in the everyday world:

>> **Control:** If you have a big multinational enterprise or a consortium, the issue of data sharing becomes fairly significant. Version control is imperfect, and it can sometimes be really difficult to tell which is the latest, most up-to-date copy.

>> **Data trustworthiness:** How do you prove if you're the creator of said data, or someone else is? What happens with corrupted data?

>> **Data monetization and transfer:** How can you transfer, buy, or sell rights to any data, and be sure that it's the only copy there is?

>> **Data changing:** How do you ensure that data is not being changed when it's not supposed to?

All these problems are solvable using cryptocurrency and blockchain. The large challenge that the industry is working through now is scaling blockchain technology to accommodate the cost and data storage demands of enterprises.

Taking Out the Third Party in Insurance

One of the greatest advantages that blockchain tech introduces into the modern finance world is the smart contracts that allow for business transactions without the involvement of a third party, such as banks or intermediaries. Removing third parties allows for things like micropayments and reduction in cost associated with repetitive human labor.

Put simply, a *smart contract* is a protocol that allows for two parties to record their transaction into a blockchain. These contracts can be used for pretty much anything, from exchange of physical goods (that have digital signatures) to exchange of information or money.

The key security feature here is that, unlike the ordinary financial database, the information is distributed to and verified by all the computers in the network, making it decentralized. The data is unique and not able to be copied; the audit trail is immutable.

Self-driving cars present a compelling use case for blockchain technology. There is a dilemma in assessing fault without a human to witness. Determining who is to blame — was it a failure of the car's navigation, a manufactured part, or the other driver?

Decentralized security

At the core of current business models is something that could be called the *centralized trust paradigm*, in which middlemen such as bankers, brokers, and lawyers coordinate and ensure the veracity of financial transactions and exchanges of goods.

Centralization comes with certain inherent security risks, such as data corruption and theft. Blockchains combat this by creating a decentralized system that is based on mutual distrust of all the participants that keep each other in check.

In order to create such a system, you create a distributed ledger that uses cryptocurrency (like Bitcoin, Ethereum, or Factom), where each participant is both the user of the system and responsible for its maintenance and upkeep.

Crowdfunded coverage

Similar to standard crowdfunding initiatives, the idea is to pool resources from numerous entities or persons in order to cover for an unexpected shortcoming in an insurance plan. For example, a retirement insurance plan could kick in only at the age of 65, but a person could be forced to retire early because of unforeseen circumstances, and additional funds would be needed by the unfortunate individual.

Economic disparity has grown over the years, and numerous underinsured or uninsured people could benefit from such a system. Crowdfunding can potentially provide benefits to all three parties in question:

>> **Insurers** gain increased revenue because more people are interested in their plans. They gain access to a greater portion of the underinsured population. In addition, the insuring company could improve its brand recognition — it could be seen as a company that cares.

>> **Donors** could benefit from possible tax exemptions, if the structure of the campaign allows it, or they could gain other benefits, such as discounts or free services.

>> **Seekers** (those looking for insurance) obviously stand to gain the most, as they can get better protection and more affordable coverage.

Cognizant proposed interesting insights to crowdfunding insurance in its white-paper. You can find it at https://goo.gl/u3Kd3U.

The implications of DAO insurance

DAOs are corporate entities that have no full-time employees, but are able to perform all the functions that a standard corporation can. The ability to create such an entity stems directly from the improvement in blockchain algorithms, which has happened over the last few years and has created what is commonly known as blockchain 2.0.

A DAO is, in essence, a form of an advanced smart contract. The DAO is able treat DAO as a corporation where all its individual policy users are shareholders, while the corporation itself never is in direct control of any particular group or individual.

In the same manner, a DAO is never under control of the developers, and they don't issue or deny policies. It's strictly a peer-to-peer insurance model. Although vulnerabilities regarding identity verification still exist, this system will be improved, and in reality, the same issues exist even in the current, centralized insurance systems.

Chapter **15**

Government

n this chapter, I introduce you to the exciting innovations that are taking place inside governments and the companies that support them with innovative blockchain projects.

Everyday business is affected by scams and fraud, and this chapter explains how governments are fighting back against cybercrime and identity theft. You also find out about smart cities initiatives, which will be critical to economic growth and sustainability — many are using blockchain technology to bridge technological gaps.

The Smart Cities of Asia

Smart cities are taking advantage of modern technology to enhance infrastructure function, and safety, and improve things like traffic and air quality. The business of becoming a smart city is booming, and almost every larger municipality has embraced the smart city concept.

Blockchain is especially useful when integrated with the Internet of Things (IoT) used by smart cities. Several interesting projects are being piloted now for commercial deployment. The U.S. Department of Homeland Security is exploring securing IoT devices used by Customs and Border Protection (CBP). Companies such as Slock.it are allowing connected objects to use the blockchain to enter into smart contracts; its first product was a blockchain-enabled smart lock, which could be used be Airbnb customers. The integration of these technologies allows devices to use their sensors to set up smart contracts. This same technology could be used by city parking meters.

Figure 15-1 shows the home page of Singapore's Smart Nation project. Singapore has been courting startups from around the world to develop new technology in its "regulatory sandbox." It's a welcome invitation to blockchain technology companies that have been operating in the *gray zone* (where there is not a clear regulatory framework established), however many countries, like Singapore are taking direct action to define the space and let companies know what is allowed and not allowed.

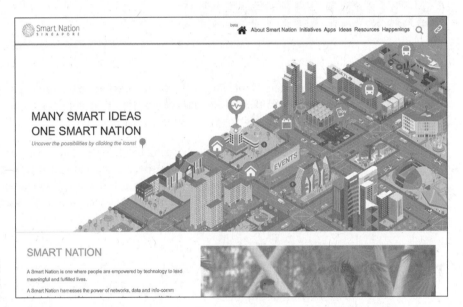

FIGURE 15-1:
Singapore's Smart Nation project.

Blockchain technology could also be used to share information between networks in a smart city securely. Many cities are exploring how to use blockchain to alleviate traffic jams. Singapore's Smart Nation project hopes to use the mobile phones of its citizens to measure the conditions of their bus rides, and then analyze the data to see when roads need to be upgraded. Singapore has been a leader in smart city development and has begun developing smart cities in other countries.

In this section, I walk you through some of the many blockchain efforts that are taking place in Asia.

Singapore satellite cities in India

The Indian government launched its Smart Cities Mission in 2015, with the intention of building 100 new smart cities. Many of these developments will be in the Delhi Mumbai Industrial Corridor, which is a 620-mile (1,000km) stretch between Delhi and Mumbai. Infrastructure worth $11 billion has already been planned across 33 cities, and much of the development will be funded through a public–private model. The project is expected to attract $90 billion in foreign investment, which will be used to create business parks, manufacturing zones and smart cities, all of which will be situated along a delegated rail freight corridor.

These smart cities are being developed as India's economy industrializes and the population becomes more urbanized. State intervention in the form of centrally planned cities is necessary in order to prevent the existing cities from becoming overcrowded and unlivable. India is particularly vulnerable to climate change because of its immense and impoverished population. Because of this, it's important that these cities are sustainable and smart. They need low-energy housing materials, intelligent grids, planned transportation, integrated IT systems, e-governance, and innovative water harvesting.

Singapore is a prime example of an intelligently planned city. Despite the high population density, it has excellent infrastructure and a high quality of life. Many of Singapore's private organizations have the knowledge and resources that are needed to develop India's smart cities. In collaboration with the Indian government, the private sector would be able to provide the capital, skills, and technology that are necessary for such large plans.

Andhara Pradesh and the Monetary Authority of Singapore have announced a financial technology (fintech) innovation partnership, with a primary focus on blockchain and digital payments. Singapore aims to develop a marketplace for fintech solutions in India.

Singaporean leadership has shown interest in partnering with India to develop a smart city as well as a new capital for Andhra Pradesh, a state in the southeast. It's setting up committees to analyze the potential for collaboration in India's plan to build 100 new cities, as well as further developing the infrastructure across 500 existing towns and cities.

India's minister of urban development has been in talks with both Singapore's current prime minister and its former prime minister. He has been seeking Singapore's expertise in smart cities, particularly focusing on intelligent transport systems, enhanced water management, and e-governance. The minister of urban development has also been examining Singapore's public housing schemes, as well as their private housing regulations. Funding structures for transport infrastructure have been looked at as well.

Indian authorities have also engaged a team of Singaporean experts to assist the development of a satellite town in Himachal Pradesh. The 49-acre (20-hectare) project aims to help decongest Shimla, a town that has had a massive population rise in the past few decades. The Singaporeans will assist in educational, residential, and commercial aspects of the town under development.

Both Singapore and Malaysia have shown interest in investing in another satellite town near Jathia Devi. The Singaporean government is undertaking a study that will assess various options. The state government of Himachal Pradesh is looking at developing five satellite towns near existing cities, using a private–public funding model.

Singapore's Ascendas-Singbridge launched its eighth IT park in India. The 59-acre (24-hectare) International Tech Park Gurgaon is expected to have its first building completed in the middle of the year. The $400 million project aims to offer 8 million square feet of business space to help accommodate India's burgeoning IT sector.

China's big data problem

Blockchain technology is widely being discussed in China as a way to enhance the reliability of big data. People are looking at it as a way to solve the trust issue involved in sharing data between two or more parties that don't have aligned incentives. Blockchain technology offers many new solutions to track ownership, origin, and authenticity.

Peernova is a promising U.S. company that is tackling big data problems. It previously focused on Bitcoin mining but pivoted into the blockchain space and raised $4 million from Zhejiang Zhongnan Holdings Groups, a construction company from China. Peernova plans to use blockchain technology to query traditional databases and track changes.

The use cases are to verify any changes to subsets of large data stores and use the more efficient and complete cryptographic audits instead of a traditional auditor to provide a reference point for a company. It hopes to help hedge funds calculate the tax liability of their investments by using blockchain to trace the history of money that has been invested over the years.

Dalian Wanda, the biggest real estate developer in China, is also getting into the blockchain game. It has teamed up with big data software company Cloudera to launch a blockchain project called Hercules. It sees the potential to use blockchain technology to make predictions derived from big data actionable for managers as they're occurring, moving managers from reactive to proactive in situations like modifications to their protocols, as well as monitor user behavior within their systems.

Dalian Wanda and Cloudera aim to keep developing Hercules and integrate their technology into a variety of industries that rely on IT and big data. Project Hercules will act as an open-source suite that supports the needs of businesses. It makes it easier for organizations to deploy and manage blockchain apps on large data clusters.

You might find it odd to see a digital mining company partner with a traditional construction company to tackle auditing issues for hedge funds, or real estate companies working with big data to solve issues for system administrators, but this is the wild west of the blockchain world. The shortage in blockchain talent and the high demand for blockchain projects and investment are fueling this environment.

The Battle for the Financial Capital of the World

Blockchain technology has come into its own since breaking into the public consciousness with a plethora of news coverage in 2015. Many startups have been working on beta and pre-launch builds since then, with nearly 2,000 new blockchain startups forming overnight in 2016. Many of these will finally go to market sometime in 2017 and 2018 in Singapore, Dubai, and London where the regulatory bodies welcome innovation and compete to be the financial mecca of the world. This isn't just about fintech and smart cities for these leaders. It's a race for relevance in a world shifting to borderless and financially fluid global citizens.

London's early foresight

In 2016, the central government of the United Kingdom put out a report called "Distributed Ledger Technology: Beyond Block Chain" (https://goo.gl/asIz6L), which asserted that distributed ledger technology (blockchains) could be used to reduce corruption, errors, and fraud, and make various processes more efficient. They also stated blockchains could change the relationship of citizens with their government by bringing about more transparency and trustworthiness. But London has been very friendly to the technology since at least 2014. Many early blockchain startups incorporated or worked in London because it was the unofficially safest place to build a business. This was a big deal at that time because many cryptocurrency entrepreneurs were being arrested in 2014 and 2015.

Since this report came out, blockchains have been approved for use across government applications in the UK, including Whitehall departments (non-ministerial departments such as Land Registry, Forestry Commission, and Food Standards), local authorities, and delegated governments.

Here are several interesting projects and experiments that are happening in the UK:

>> **Blockchain-based welfare distribution:** The Department of Work and Pensions has partnered with Barclays, RWE, GovCoin, and the University of London in an experiment that will use blockchain technology to distribute welfare with a phone app. The trial was designed to see if payments could be sent and tracked using blockchain technology.

>> **Government DLT:** Credits, a blockchain platform provider, and the UK government are collaborating on a framework that allows UK government agencies to experiment with blockchain technology. (DLT stands for distributed ledger technology.)

>> **Blockchain-based international payments:** Santander Bank has launched a trial of blockchain-based international payments. The staff pilot program involves an app that connects to Apple Pay. Users can use touch ID to transfer payments of between £10 and £10,000.

>> **Using blockchain technology to trade gold:** The Royal Mint has teamed up with CME Group, a market operator, to use blockchain technology to build a gold market in the hopes of making London a more appealing city for gold sales. Blockchain technology is being adopted by the two entities because they see it as an efficient digital mechanism for trading gold.

These are all experiments to see if blockchain technology is the new platform to exchange value. The success or failure of this scheme will define the future course of the UK and the rest of the world.

The regulatory sandbox of Singapore

Singapore, like the UK, has gone out of its way to make working there as easy, friendly, and financially appealing as possible. In 2015, government officials traveled to San Francisco to announce and recruit entrepreneurs to come work in what they coined a "regulatory sandbox" — a play on the term *development sandbox*, which is a safe environment where developers can build software. Singapore had the same idea in mind for building software companies.

At that time, blockchain companies in the United States and many other places were still in the gray zone. The idea of a safe place to operate and invest money was very appealing to many entrepreneurs, myself included. If you've never been to Singapore, you should go! It's beautiful, clean, and safe.

Singapore is taking steps to explore the technology, and it's paying off. A Singaporean bank, OCBC, used blockchain technology for cross-border transfers. It sent money to its subsidiaries, OCBC Malaysia and the Bank of Singapore.

R3 has also been active in Singapore. It opened an lab for researching and developing digital ledger technologies alongside Monetary Authority of Singapore. R3 is working on an exchange to support interbank payments. The banks will deposit cash and be issued a digital currency.

Singapore's central bank also launched a pilot project, along with eight foreign and local banks as well as the stock exchange. This proof-of-concept project aims to use the blockchain technology for its interbank payments. The pilot project also aims to review cross-border foreign currency transactions.

It's not just blockchain companies that are going to experiment in Singapore. All the biggest players have gotten involved — Bank of America, Merrill Lynch, IBM, Credit Suisse, The Bank of Tokyo-Mitsubishi UFJ Ltd, DBS Bank Ltd, JP Morgan, The Hong Kong and Shanghai Banking Corp Ltd, OCBC Bank, United Overseas Bank, and the Singapore Exchange.

TIP

Every bank in the world must know who it's doing business with. The whole idea of know your customer (KYC) helps combat money laundering and tourist funding.

The next phase will be determining foreign currency transactions and building on Singapore's KYC efforts. This could lead to the country forging the way in blockchain-based identity. Singapore already has a robust and modern digital identity system that could easily be connected to a blockchain.

The Dubai 2020 initiative

The government of Dubai has an ambitious plan to move all government documents and systems onto the blockchain by 2020. The scheme to go paperless is part of its initiative to become a global leader in blockchain technology and boost efficiency across all sectors.

The Minister of Cabinet Affairs and the Future detailed how the new scheme will enable users to update and verify their credentials through the blockchain. They'll only have to log in with their credentials once to have access to both government and private entities, such as insurance companies and banks. They also anticipate sharing their technology with other countries to allow simpler border crossings. Instead of passports, travelers could use pre-authenticated digital wallets, as well as pre-approved identification.

The Dubai government has estimated that its blockchain initiative has the potential to save 25.1 million hours in productivity. This boost in efficiency will also help to cut back on carbon emissions.

Dubai's Global Blockchain Council (GBC) announced seven new public-private collaborations, combining the skills and resources of startups, local businesses, and government departments. They'll apply blockchain technology to the following:

>> **Healthcare:** The Estonian software company, Guardtime will collaborate with one of Dubai's largest telecom operators, Du, to provide the technological expertise for digitizing healthcare records and moving them to the blockchain.

>> **The diamond trade:** A pilot project will use blockchain technology for the authentication and transfer of diamonds. The Dubai Multi Commodities Center will be digitize *Kimberly certificates* (documents created by the UN to restrict the trade of conflict diamonds).

>> **Title transfers:** Title transfers will be digitized and recorded on a blockchain. A Singaporean blockchain startup known as Dxmarkets has developed a proof-of-concept.

- » **Business registration:** The GBC is trialing the use of blockchain technology for business registration. This is different from the decentralized autonomous organization (DAO) of Ethereum but could streamline identity verification through the Flexi Desk program. It's currently in the demo stage, with several entities working on a proof-of-concept.

- » **Tourism:** Dubai Points is a pilot program that was launched in collaboration with Loyyal, using blockchain technology to help the tourism industry. It aims to incentivize travel by granting points to travelers who visit certain places. It will use smart contracts to facilitate the rewards. These points many work like a crypto token and be tradable an exchanges.

- » **Shipping:** IBM is working with the GBC to use blockchain technology for improved shipping and logistics. The program aims to help regional players to collaborate on how they exchange goods. Smart contracts will be utilized as solutions for compliance and settlement issues.

Dubai, like Singapore, has put its money and talent into insuring that it will dominate the blockchain space quickly. This is one luxury of small government and central authority.

Bitlicense regulatory framework: New York City

If you're planning on operating a blockchain startup in New York City, plan for extra fees. In June 2015, the New York State Department of Financial Services (NYDFS) put out the final version of Bitlicense, the regulatory framework for digital currency aimed to give the industry more clarity. In reality, it pushed many blockchain startups out of NYC. The license itself costs $5,000 and can be up to 500 pages. It requires the fingerprints of each company's leaders and an extensive background check on the applying businesses. The chief complaint is the roughly $100,000 in expenses associated with the application. This estimate includes time allocation, legal, and compliance fees. Bitlicense is in stark contrast to the efforts made by other financial centers such and London, Singapore, and Dubai.

The final Bitlicense was the result of almost two years of research and debate over how the technology should be regulated. It came about after it was deemed that the existing regulations were not suitable for digital currency companies.

On a positive note, NYC blockchain businesses no longer need approval from the NYDFS for new software updates or further rounds of venture capital funding. The framework states that digital currency firms only need approval for changes that are "proposed to an existing product, service, or activity that may cause such product, service, or activity to be materially different from that previously listed on the application for licensing by the superintendent."

The first company to receive a Bitlicense was Circle, the Bitcoin wallet providers. The license allows them to operate in New York under the regulatory framework. Circle is one of the few companies that can legally do so. Most blockchain startups are avoiding working in New York because the cost and effort of the license outweigh the benefit. Only the highest-funded startups are making an effort.

Ripple has been awarded its second license. This iteration of their license has allowed it to sell and hold XRP, which is the digital asset behind the Ripple Consensus Ledger (RCL). It will enhance Ripple's ability to deal with business customers who want to use its technology for international funds transfers.

Other U.S. regions have also put up similar bills to regulate digital currency and require licensing. California bill AB 1326, would have done that for the region but failed after the Electronic Frontier Foundation (EFF) was able to oppose it. (The EFF is a group based in San Francisco that defends consumer rights and new technology.)

Friendly legal structure of Malta

European Union member country Malta has taken drastic and direct steps to embrace blockchain technology. Moving much more quickly than other nations, Malta saw the potential of blockchain and took steps to secure itself as a hub for innovation. Most blockchain startups have faced a hostile environment, so many — including the mega-exchange Binance — have flocked to Malta to set up business.

After the United Kingdom exits the EU, Malta will be one of the few countries left in the EU that has English as an official language. Malta is also governed by continental law and common law, which makes them more favorable to business. This has positioned Malta well to support international blockchain and cryptocurrency-related companies that want to incorporate and have a legal structure.

Malta as a small island that has seen many different ruling regimes. Each established their own rules and some of them have stuck. Malta has a mixed legal framework now that includes Roman law, French law, British law, and their own laws enacted by the Maltese parliament after the 1964 Independence. But they are mostly known for civil or continental law (which has been codified over the years) and common law (which is established through court rulings).

Malta has passed two groundbreaking acts and one bill that have shifted the conversation around legal standing for blockchain companies, offering legal protection and a framework that more accurately governs distributed technology, blockchains, and all the innovation that has grown out of them. Here's a summary of these three pieces of legislation:

» **Virtual Financial Assets Act:** The Virtual Financial Assets Act regulates initial coin offerings (ICOs). The law requires any company raising capital through an ICO to publish a white paper giving a detailed description of the whole project. The ICO must also make the company's financial history public.

» **Malta Digital Innovation Authority Act:** The Malta Digital Innovation Authority Act creates regulatory procedures for cryptocurrency and the blockchain companies. It also establishes a regulatory body called the Malta Digital Innovation Authority (MDIA).

» **Technology Arrangements and Services Bill:** The Technology Arrangements and Services Bill allows blockchain companies and cryptocurrency exchanges to register and be certified by the Malta government.

These new acts and bill have open up Malta to new technology and will possibly be used as an example by other governments that also hope to attract innovation. The greatest benefit is giving companies a safe place to grow and experiment within known parameters.

Securing the World's Borders

Blockchain is being explored by many governments to secure borders. The UK has an ambitious goal of ensuring that travelers never need to break stride as they move through their airports. This is in contrast to the long security lines that are present now at almost every airport. The main hurdles that the UK must overcome for frictionless travel experience have to do with *passenger resolution* (the ability to know definitively any given passenger's identity, even if the passenger is from another country). Passenger resolution has been a problem for countries that are fighting terrorism.

The United States has opened up its technology for passenger resolution under the Global Travel Assessment System (GTAS). It's available for public collaboration on GitHub (www.github.com/US-CBP/GTAS).

Computers, cameras, and sensors involved in the noninvasive screening and authentication of passengers all need to be secured to ensure national security. Blockchains, with their underlying immutable properties, are a promising technology for this use case and are being tested now.

The other interesting thing that can be created through blockchains is biographical identities — identities that are built over time. Any data can be linked with a biographical identity, and the privacy and readability of the attributed data can be managed by publishers. Over time, identity is built by adding additional attributes. Attributes can be just about anything, from data off your personal device to instances that your documents were checked at a border crossing. These attributes are published to the individual's chain of identity by certificate authorities or those authorized by certificate authorities.

The Department of Homeland Security and the identity of things

The Department of Homeland Security under the Science and Technology Directorate is exploring securing IoT devices for the U.S. borders. It's working with Factom, Inc., an Austin, Texas–based blockchain startup to advance the security of digital identity for IoT devices.

Factom creates identity logs that captures the ID of a device, who manufactured it, lists of available updates, known security issues, and granted authorities while adding the dimension of time for added security. The goal is to limit would-be hackers' abilities to corrupt the past records for a device, making it harder to spoof.

Passports of the future

ShoCard (www.shocard.com) is an application development company that is working with the blockchain company Blockcypher. It has built prototypes that allow you to establish your identity within a secure blockchain environment. ShoCard ID lives on an app on your phone and can be used to share all different kinds of credentials securely.

The new feeder document

You may not have heard of Smartrac, but it's more than likely that you touch a piece of its technology every day. Smartrac is the number-one provider of radio-frequency identification (RFID) tags and other identification chips that live inside of things like passports and ID cards.

One of the largest challenges that countries face while fighting identity fraud is in the authentication of the underlying documents used to build identities. These are things like Social Security cards, birth certificates, and diplomas, which are currently easy and cheap to knock off.

Smartrac has been battling this problem with more and more sophisticated technology. Its latest innovation, dLoc, is a software authentication solution that allows feeder documents to be checked against a blockchain record.

Document data is married to a unique ID of the near-field communication tag (NFC) to create a 32-bit hash value, which is only recognizable by the issuing agency using a private key. The hash value is stored in Smart Cosmos and backed up in a public blockchain. After that has happened, the document with the dLoc sticker can be verified using a desktop reader or a mobile app on an NFC-enabled phone.

What this does is create a two amazing things that have never been possible with paper documents:

>> An unalterable history of the document, showing its true age and ownership.

>> Allowing certificate authorities to sign for the authenticity of a document cryptographically. So, even if the underlying paper used to create documents was stolen, it would not be adequately signed, or if a document was taken after it was issued, it could be marked as a stolen document.

Chapter **16**

Other Industries

t's easy to focus on the most prominent blockchain projects and industry impacts, but blockchain technology has already begun to touch all aspects of society.

In this chapter, I lead you through some of the more interesting and unusual applications of blockchain technology that you may not have suspected. Some of the most exciting transformations will occur within government systems, new trust layers for the Internet, and new industries created by blockchains. Here, you discover the most impressive changes that are taking place now and how these transformations will affect your life and the industry you work in, as well as the governments and agencies that protect you.

Lean Governments

A few small nations have realized that if they are going to compete in a global economy, they have to offer more and do it in a way that does not burden their citizens. In order to compete, they've shifted many of the traditional ideas around what it means to provide citizenship. In a world that is moving from hard borders to very porous ones, where people have the power to choose where they live and what country they call home, these small countries are doing well.

Citizenship is becoming a commodity that can be purchased, with each nation offering different advantages. Countries are moving away from the passive citizenship model, where you're born a citizen of a country, to one where you choose citizenship based on the advantages that that country offers.

Under this new model, citizenship is no longer tied to a physical location. Government can exist without borders or a physical location. Old models see citizenship as a location that can be invaded and overruled by another nation or sources within, such as a revolution.

Blockchain technology and other top-grade innovations are being embraced in these areas — first, because they makes it possible and, second, because they help reduce the weight on government by creating more efficient systems that citizens can access quickly anywhere in the world, even if the physical territory is overrun.

Singapore, Estonia, the United Arab Emirates (UAE), and China have all been market leaders in these types of initiatives. The Smart Nation project of Singapore and e-Residency of Estonia are unique systems that strive to reduce the paperwork and wait times of citizens and increase the efficiency of shared resources. The 2020 initiative that Dubai launched will remove all physical documents and replace them with blockchain-backed documents or systems. China's efforts to reduce fraud have changed the dynamics for the blockchain space.

Singapore's Smart Nation project

Smart Nation is Singapore's national effort to create a future of better living for all its citizens and inhabitants. People, businesses, and government are working together. The project spans from digital identity all the way to IoT sensors that optimize public records.

Singapore believes that people empowered by technology can lead more meaningful and fulfilled lives. It's exploiting new technologies, networks, and big data to its fullest and actively seeking innovation through regulator sandboxes and active recruitment and incentivizing innovation by startups.

You can see a depiction of the Smart Nation initiative at https://goo.gl/EGmF4X.

Singapore has been able to quickly test and deploy new technology because it has a single layer government. It coordinates policies and efforts across institutions quickly. Smart Nation is an excellent example of this philosophy that new technology trumps politics as usual.

Estonia's e-Residency

Estonia is a small country in the European Union with 1.3 million inhabitants. It has limited resources to meet the needs of its citizens, but through technology, it has been able to exceed the capabilities of many larger nations. Estonia launched digital ID cards for online services and was the first country to offer *e-Residency*, a digital identity, available to anyone in the world interested in operating a business online.

Signing up for an Estonia e-Residency takes a few minutes, and the background check costs about $100. Having an e-Residency card does not make you a citizen of Estonia, but it does give you a lot of benefits.

TIP

You can also become an Estonia e-Resident. Apply online at `https://apply.gov.ee`.

After it exited the Soviet Union, Estonia invested heavily in new technology. It shifted completely away from traditional government to one where it utilizes a *single-window principle* (one point of access for citizens). The single-window principle enables access to all tax and customs services for citizens with a single secure log-in anywhere in the world. Straightforward and paper-free transactions are made possible through this system. Everything, except marriage and real estate purchases, can be done completely online. Estonian citizens can make bank transfers or pay tax in a few minutes.

The Estonian people have come to expect their government to simplify and use more IT solutions. The active development of e-services has reduced the number of visits to the Estonian Tax and Customs Board service bureaus by more than 60 percent between 2009 and 2016, lowering the overall cost.

Estonia upgraded its income and social tax returns environment in 2015 and collected €125 million more in value-added tax (VAT) than the previous year due to the development and extensive usage of e-services. The Estonian government added a tax liability calculator that pulls data from incorporated banking systems of citizens. It also made it easy to submit invoices to the system.

The Estonians have embraced blockchain technologies. The next big development will be a blockchain-enabled cloud. Estonia has hired Ericsson, Apcera, and Guardtime to jointly develop and operate a hybrid cloud platform that will enhance the scalability, resilience, and data security of tax reporting and online health care advice.

Nasdaq is developing blockchain services in Estonia as well. It's building a market for private companies that keeps track of the shares they issue and enables them to settle transactions immediately. It's focused on improving the proxy voting process for enterprises. It will be a way to register your business.

The Bitnation project is collaborating with Estonia to offer a public notary to Estonian e-Residents, which will allow Estonia's e-Residents, regardless of where they live or do business, to notarize their marriages, birth certificates, and business contracts on a blockchain. Blockchain notarized documents aren't legally binding in the Estonian jurisdiction, or in any other nation or state, but it will allow citizens to prove the age of these documents.

Better notarization in China

China has a love–hate relationship with cryptocurrency. On the one hand, Chinese citizens have been trying to use tokens as a means to launder money out of the country or hide profits from taxation. This has caused the Chinese government to tighten regulation around the use of cryptocurrencies. However, as the usefulness of the underlying blockchain technology has expanded beyond the movement of value, China has begun to embrace blockchain technology.

An interesting example of its early use was by Ancun Zhengxin Co., which is leading the shift to electronic data notarization services in China through partnerships with more than 100 traditional notarial offices in 28 provinces. It's also offering electronic data storage and blockchain notarization solution through traditional offices.

Ancun publishes thousands of records in a publicly searchable blockchain that allow users to go back and check the authenticity and age of notarized documents.

TIP

Many startups are working on similar concepts in the United States. For example, Tierion (www.tierion.com) lets you hash and timestamp date; it anchors the data for you in the Bitcoin blockchain.

The Trust Layer for the Internet

Over the last 30 years, the Internet has been built in layers — one layer on top of the next — making it easier and safer for the those using it. The blockchain is the next layer of the Internet. Think of it as the trust layer. It will likely fade quietly out of the public's consciousness and just start making your online interactions more pleasant. The implementation of blockchain technology will eventually do away with irritating problems that commonly occur online because there aren't sufficient ways to trust information.

There are two key areas where work has begun that you may not be aware of but will love: email with little to no spam and a new kind of identity online.

Spam-free email

You likely hate spam as much as I do, but there is a bigger problem than too many unwanted emails. The current email systems are no longer secure. At the end of 2016, Yahoo! suffered one of the world's largest hacks. One billion user accounts were compromised, and users' personal data was exposed.

Securing email is a compelling use case for blockchain technology, and email is ready to be disrupted. A legend in online security has taken on the challenge. Dr. John McAfee, the antivirus software pioneer, has created a new platform for email based on blockchain technology.

John McAfee SwiftMail (`www.johnmcafeeswiftmail.com`) is a blockchain-based email. It isn't that different from the email systems you're used to. It's easy to navigate, and some developers have built mobile apps and web-based apps to make the experience more convenience.

SwiftMail's blockchain confirms that your mail is genuine and that the emails you send were received by the intended parties, removing the need to trust a third party, like Yahoo!, with your data. There is also a small inherent cost to send an email that desensitizes spammers.

SwiftMail takes a strong stance on privacy where many service providers have a blasé attitude. John McAfee says, "If privacy doesn't matter, would you be willing to give your wallet to a total stranger and let them go through it and write down everything they find inside? Then why on earth would we believe that if we're not doing anything wrong, we shouldn't care if someone has our information?"

SwiftMail uses wallet address similar to a Bitcoin wallet that is kept on an application on your computer. They are 32 random characters with no metadata to scrap, and users can create new ones quickly, just as you do with Bitcoin. The emails themselves are 256-bit, end-to-end encryption making intercepted data useless to thieves.

Currently, downloads for SwiftMail are only available for Android, Linux and Windows systems. There is no Apple-friendly version of this software yet. Don't download the wrong version.

Other projects in this space, including Earn (`https://earn.com`), are working on giving email a blockchain backend. They've created email that charges people outside your network a fee to send you email. Then they give you the option to keep the money or donate it to charity.

Owning your identity

One of the fundamental tenets that blockchain enthusiast talks about is the personal responsibility of owning the data that you create and that identifies you uniquely. This concept might seem straightforward, but most people don't own or control the data that represents their identities.

Most of the control is held by centralized databases that are vulnerable to hacking. These databases hold the information, and certificate authorities validate that the information is correct and unaltered. In the information age, your data is your identity. The more distributed the data is, the higher the likelihood that it will fall into the hands of those who want to misuse it.

Blockchain-based identity places control of identity in the hands of the individuals or corporations that the identity represents. Central databases and certificate authorities are not necessarily replaced. Data still needs a secure home, and it still makes sense to have third parties validate the authenticity of documents.

The value in changing the order of responsibility around identity is that it becomes harder to steal, hold hostage, or manipulate the underlying documents that represent your identity. Information is shared as needed without exposing unnecessary information. An irrevocable and globally accessible identity may not always be a good thing. Those building identity platforms will need to be mindful of consumer protection such as credit forgiveness, the right to be forgotten, and voter anonymity.

Oracle of the Blockchain

Blockchain technology doesn't solve for the problem that information must come from somewhere. It's also important that the information can be relied on. It's the human element that can't yet be removed from the equation when you want to act on a contract within a blockchain system.

There is no central authority to police or enforce honesty in a blockchain system. Predicting the future honesty of authors of information is impossible. The logical conclusion is that each transaction must cost less than the cost to rebuild reputation. The reputations of trusted authors are built over time, and the longer an author is honest and correct, the more valuable the author's reputation becomes. This concept is similar to the value of a name brand.

In this section, I explain how artists and creatives are using blockchain technology to monetize their work through blockchain technology.

Trusted authorship

Smart contracts and chain codes have created a new opportunity for knowledgeable individuals and corporations to monetize their information. These types of systems need trusted sources of information to execute against. These trusted sources could be rating agencies, weather outlets, or just about anything else.

You could also connect IoT devices to a blockchain infrastructure and have them create their own voices and identities on a blockchain network. They need to build trust over time and can still be corrupted at any given point. Past honesty doesn't prevent future dishonesty or the corruption of a source of information.

Not all smart contracts or chain codes are self-contained or execute against infallible sources. The more practical and applicable business use case requires information to be derived from sources outside the known universe of any given blockchain network. Several startups are attacking this problem from different angles.

Po.et is a startup that is building a decentralized protocol for content ownership, discovery, and monetization. Its system is designed to record and timestamp metadata and ownership information about creative assets, such as writing and music.

Factom has created Acolyte, a service that allows users to build a reputation over time for the information they provide to the network. Smart contract builders can subscribe and compensate oracles that are created. They can also rate them for their trustworthiness.

From a dramatically different angle, Augur, another blockchain startup, has pioneered the idea of prediction markets. Augur is a platform that rewards users for predicting future real-world events such as election or corporate buyouts. The bets are made by trading virtual shares in the outcome of events. Users make money by buying shares in the correct outcomes. The cost of the shares fluctuates based on how the community feels about the likelihood of the event acutely happening. Augur is similar to a betting website. Anyone can make a prediction. Anyone can create a prediction market for any given event. This would allow you as a business owner, for example, to take a poll on what people think is most likely to occur. It may also uncover inside information that authors would like to be able to capitalize on.

Intellectual property rights

One of the hardest-hit industries that is struggling with intellectual property rights is the music industry. Artists at the top are squeezed out economically by the many intermediaries that rely on their creative work. Small artists can't make music a primary source of income because they only see a small fraction of the revenue. Mega-stars make it on the sheer volume of fans.

The Internet has made it easier for artists of all sizes to share their work. At the same time, it has made it even harder for people to make a comfortable living doing what they love. The music industry food chain is a long, and each intermediary takes a small piece of the pie and adds to the length of time that it takes for funds to finally reach the artist. Often, the artist will wait up to 18 months or more to see any money and may only get $0.000035 per instance of her music being streamed. This situation is a best-case scenario in our current market, with no one defrauding the artist.

Blockchain has been introduced as a way to help lighten the massive financial burden on creatives. Cryptocurrency could be used to reduce transaction fees associated with credit cards and fraud. It would also open up new markets in developing countries that don't have regular access to credit cards.

An even more interesting but less straightforward possibility would be migrating the whole music industry ecosystem onto a blockchain system that utilized smart contracts or chain code to facilitate immediate payment for utilization. It could also clarify ownership of licenses and make it easier for consumers to license music for commercial use.

Several projects are working on this issue and looking to promote a healthy, sustainable, and frictionless ecosystem — one that does not displace market player but does allow artists to gain a bit more from their hard work.

UjoMusic is beta testing its platform that lets users sell and license music directly. It utilizes the Ethereum network, smart contracts for execution, and Ether (the Ethereum cryptocurrency) for payment. You can download a whole song or just the vocal and instrumental stems for commercial or noncommercial use. The musicians are then paid immediately with Ether.

Peertracks is another blockchain startup that's working on changing the music industry. It's a music streaming website that allows users to download and discover new artists. It does this through its peer-to-peer network called MUSE and the creation of individual artist tokens. These tokens work like other cryptocurrency and fluctuate in value depending on the popularity of the artist.

Blockchain technology doesn't remove the need for music labels and distributors. However, they'll need to act quickly if they don't want to be displaced by new companies that adapt this more efficient model, just as Netflix disrupted Blockbuster.

5

The Part of Tens

Discover ten free blockchain resources that will help you stay up to speed on the technology and the industry.

Identify ten rules to never break while working within the cryptocurrency and blockchain world.

Find out more on the top ten blockchain projects and organizations that are shaping the future of the industry.

Chapter **17**

Ten (Or So) Free Blockchain Resources

In this chapter, I outline interesting free resources across the blockchain ecosystem that will help you stay informed and get involved in the community. Here, you can find free tools for making *oracles* (the data feeds that allow smart contracts to execute), videos that will expand your knowledge, and organizations that are shaping the future of the industry.

Ethereum

Ethereum is an open-source crowdfunded project that built the Ethereum blockchains. It's one of the most important projects in the space because it has pioneered building a programing language within a blockchain. Due to its built-in programing language, the Ethereum network allows you to create smart contracts, create decentralized organizations, and deploy decentralized applications.

Ethereum 101 (www.ethereum.org) is a website started by the members of the Ethereum community. It's a curated repository for high-quality educational content about blockchain technology and the Ethereum network. Anthony D'Onofrio, Ethereum's Director of Community, oversees the project.

DigiKnow

DigiByte is a decentralized payment network inspired by Bitcoin. It allows you to move money over the Internet and offers faster transactions and lower fees than Bitcoin. The network is also open to those who want to mine its native token.

The founder of DigiByte, Jared Tate, created a video series on YouTube, called DigiKnow, that teaches you just about everything you need to know to utilize DigiByte. Here is a link to his first video, where he walks you through the basics of how blockchains work and how the DigiByte network adds value: `https://youtu.be/scr6BzFddso`.

Blockchain University

Blockchain University is an educational website that teaches developers, manager, and entrepreneurs about the blockchain ecosystem. It offers public and private training programs, hackathons, and demo events. Its programs are solution-oriented design thinking and hands-on experiential training. You can find Blockchain University in Mountain View, California, or at `https://theblockchainu.com` and `https://dlt.education`.

Bitcoin Core

Bitcoin Core (`https://bitcoin.org`) was originally used by Satoshi Nakamoto to host his whitepaper on Bitcoin protocol. It's home to educational material on Bitcoin core protocol and downloadable versions of the original Bitcoin software.

The site is dedicated to keeping Bitcoin decentralized and accessible to the average person.

REMEMBER

It's a community-run project, and not all the content is managed by the core team. Keep this in mind while perusing the site.

Blockchain Alliance

The Blockchain Alliance was founded by the Blockchain Chamber of Digital Commerce and the news organization Coincenter. It's a public-private collaboration by the blockchain community, law enforcement, and regulators. They share a common goal to make the blockchain ecosystem more secure and to promote further development of technology. They do this by combat criminal activity on the blockchain by providing education, technical assistance, and periodic informational sessions regarding Bitcoin and other digital currencies and those utilize blockchain technology.

You can learn more about their events or join their organization at `www.blockchainalliance.org`.

Multichain Blog

Multichain is a company that helps organizations rapidly build applications on blockchains. They offer a platform that can issue millions of assets on a private blockchain and you can also track and verify activity on your network through their tools. Beyond their toolset and platform, they've been thought leaders in the blockchain space.

These are my favorite posts from their blog (`www.multichain.com/blog`):

>> Four genuine blockchain use cases (`www.multichain.com/blog/2016/05/four-genuine-blockchain-use-cases/`)

>> Beware the impossible smart contract (`www.multichain.com/blog/2016/04/beware-impossible-smart-contract/`)

>> Smart contracts and the DAO implosion (`www.multichain.com/blog/2016/06/smart-contracts-the-dao-implosion/`)

>> Understanding zero knowledge blockchains (`www.multichain.com/blog/2016/11/understanding-zero-knowledge-blockchains/`)

HiveMind

Paul Sztorc founded Truthcoin, a peer-to-peer oracle system and prediction marketplace for Bitcoin. It utilizes a proof-of-work sidechain that stores data on the state of prediction markets. Bitcoin can support financial derivatives and smart contracts through HiveMind, the platform developed out of the Truthcoin whitepaper. Check out their resources and education materials at `http://bitcoinhivemind.com`.

Smith + Crown

Smith + Crown is a blockchain research organization focusing on global trends, industry intelligence, and blockchain systems structure. They've created research tools to expand blockchain companies. Smith + Crown looks for impact, application, and accessibility. They've made most of their research publicly available and free of charge. You can take advantage of the research tools, countless reports, and databases of all noteworthy projects in the blockchain space. Smith + Crown are the researchers and advisors to several prominent blockchains and cryptocurrency advocacy groups, such as the Chamber for Digital Commerce, the Token Alliance, and Social Alpha. Check them out at `https://www.smithandcrown.com`.

Unchained and Unconfirmed Podcasts

The *Unchained* and *Unconfirmed* podcasts are amazing and up-to-date interviews with top industry folks in the blockchain and cryptocurrency space. *Unchained* is a weekly, hour-long podcast by Laura Shin, a former senior editor of *Forbes* and the first mainstream reporter to cover crypto assets full-time. Shin does impressive and well-thought-out deep dives into the people and companies building the decentralized Internet. She can help you get a better understanding of regulation, security, and privacy issues that are inherent in blockchain technology. You can listen to her podcast at `https://unchainedpodcast.com`.

Here are a few good episodes to listen to:

>> **Ledger on How Consumers and Institutions Should Be Safeguarding Their Private Keys:** `https://unchainedpodcast.com/ledger-on-how-consumers-and-institutions-should-be-safeguarding-their-private-keys-ep-101/`

>> **How Donating Crypto Can Help You Save on Taxes:** `https://unchained podcast.com/how-donating-crypto-can-help-you-save-on-taxes-ep-94/`

>> **Naval Ravikant On How Crypto Is Squeezing VCs, Hindering Regulators, and Bringing Users Choice:** `https://unchainedpodcast.com/naval-ravikant-on-how-crypto-is-squeezing-vcs-hindering-regulators-and-bringing-users-choice/`

>> **How Binance Became the Most Popular Crypto Exchange in 5 Months:** `https://unchainedpodcast.com/how-binance-became-the-most-popular-crypto-exchange-in-5-months-ep-84/`

Chapter **18**

The Ten Rules to Never Break on the Blockchain

I n this chapter, I dig into the things you should take into account while working with blockchain technology and the cryptocurrencies that run them.

Always consult your CPA and attorney before making financial decisions. This technology is new, and the rules that govern it are not fully developed.

REMEMBER

Don't Use Cryptocurrency or Blockchains to Skirt the Law

The legality and the legal zoning of cryptocurrencies are still fluctuating in many places of the world. I'm not kidding when I tell you to talk to your CPA and your attorney. It will be money well spent and will keep you out of trouble.

Here are three very silly questions that I get asked frighteningly often:

> » **Can I use cryptocurrency as a way to hide money?** This idea is a dangerous one. *Remember:* Blockchains keep records of all transactions forever, so even

if you think you came up with a clever way to hide some tokens, those looking for bad behavior have time to find it.

>> **Can I use blockchains as a way to smuggle money out of my country?** Many countries have limitations on the funds citizens can take out of the country. You don't want to do this for the same reason as I just mentioned: Blockchains keep records of all transactions forever.

>> **Can I use cryptocurrency to buy illicit goods?** The answer is — you guessed it — no! Blockchains keep a trail of your actions *forever!* Even law enforcement that stole Bitcoin from the infamous Silk Road marketplace got caught.

Don't do anything with cryptocurrency and blockchains that would be illegal to do with real money.

REMEMBER

Keep Your Contracts as Simple as Possible

Decentralized autonomous organizations (DAOs), smart contracts, and chaincode are all the rage at the moment. The promise of cutting administration and legal cost is very enticing to many corporations. A sometimes overlooked characteristic of this technology is that it is just code. That means that there is no human being interpreting the rules that you've laid out for everyone to follow. The code becomes law, and the law only stretches to what is incorporated into the blockchain contract. The "fat" that was cut can sometimes be very important.

There is no one to interpret the code. That means that if the code is executed in a fashion that you did not expect, there is also no one to enforce the intent of the contract. The code is law and nothing unlawful occurred. That's why you should to keep your contracts simple and modular in nature to contain and predict the outcomes of contract fulfillment. It's also a good idea to have your contract tested and beaten up even by other developers who are incentivized to break it.

The reach of the blockchain you're building your project on matters, too. You can think of it like jurisdictions. Sure, a smart contract can execute on outside data, but the smart contract cannot demand funds from accounts that they do not have access to. That means that all the value must be set aside in some manner, which may encumber cash flow.

Another thing to think about is the source of information that your contract uses to execute against. If it's weather data for an insurance contract, do you trust and agree on the source? Is it possible to manipulate the source data? A lot of thought should go into the oracle source before implementation. When building a smart contract keep in mind that your data channels may be dynamic. For example, APIs are updated frequently, and if your contract is calling one that has changed it may break your smart contract.

Publish with Great Caution

The whole point of blockchains is that once data is put in, it's hard to take it out. That means that what you put in will be around for a long time. If you publish encrypted sensitive information, you need to be okay with the fact that the encrypted data may one day be broken and what you published may be readable to anyone.

TIP

Think about this before you publish:

>> Would I be comfortable with this information being decrypted at some point?

>> Am I comfortable sharing this information for all eternity with anyone who wants to review it?

>> Is this data harmful to a third party and something that I could be liable for if published?

There is work being done in cryptography to make quantum proof encryption, but because both quantum computing and quantum proof encryption are still in the testing phase, it's difficult to say what the technology will be capable of 20 years from now.

Back Up, Back Up, Back Up Your Private Keys

REMEMBER

Blockchains are very unforgiving creatures. They don't care if you lost your private keys or passwords. Many a crypto nerd has been laid bare and given up countless tokens to the great blockchain oceans — treasure that will never be recovered.

The private keys that control your cryptocurrency often live inside your wallets, so it's important to protect and secure them. Be careful with online services that store your money for you. Many cryptocurrency exchanges and online wallets have had their funds stolen. Also, taking a screenshot or image and storing it on the cloud is the same thing as sending yourself an email. Whatever you do, do *not* do this. It will compromise your keys. You should make a plan so your loved ones can access your keys should something happen to you. A healthy 30-year-old CEO of a cryptocurrency exchange died and locked up $190 million worth of assets because he did not have a succession plan. Also, don't overlook Bluetooth connectivity as a hidden door to your cold storage. Make sure your device is completely inaccessible from the Internet.

TIP

Only store small amounts of tokens for everyday use online or in an Internet-accessible device. Think of cryptocurrency wallets like your cash wallet. Don't keep more money in it than you're willing to lose at any given time. More than a hundred known malware applications are looking to get ahold of your private keys and steal your tokens.

Keep the rest of your currency in *cold storage* — completely offline with zero access to the Internet. This could be in a paper wallet, on a computer that can't access the Internet, or in a unique hardware device built for securing cryptocurrency.

If you choose to use a paper wallet to secure your cryptocurrency, laminate it and make copies. Also keep in mind that printers often have access to the Internet and their data can be retrieved by third parties. The truly paranoid only use printers that have no access to the web. Keep your paper wallet copies in different locations such as a bank vault and a secure location in your home.

REMEMBER

Back up your digital wallets and store them in a safe place. A backup is in case your computer fails, or you make a mistake and delete the wrong file. The backup will allow you to recover your wallet in case your device was corrupted or stolen. Also, don't forget to encrypt your wallet. Encrypting your wallet allows you to set a password for withdrawing tokens.

WARNING

Encryption is a helpful measure to protect you against thieves, but it can't shield you against keylogging software. Always use a secure password that contains letters, numbers, punctuation marks, and is at least 16 characters long. The most secure passwords are those generated by programs designed specifically for that purpose. Strong passwords are harder to remember. You might consider writing down your password and laminating it like your private keys. There are limited password recovery options within cryptocurrency, and a forgotten password could mean lost tokens.

TOOLS TO KEEP YOUR TOKENS SAFE

You might consider using the BitGo wallet to secure your Bitcoin. Although it is an online wallet, BitGo requires both an online and offline signature to move your tokens. Because of this functionality, it's more secure than your standard online wallet.

BitGo wallets use three keys. They hold one, you hold one, and the other is held on your behalf by a third-party key recovery service (KRS). Two signatures are required on every transaction. Usually this is done by BitGo and you, unless you lose one of your keys; in that case, the KRS will help out. The BitGo wallet is not free — they require a small fee per transaction.

Check out the BitGo wallet at www.bitgo.com/wallet.

Triple-Check the Address Before Sending Currency

Cryptocurrency has attracted a fair number of scoundrels, so be careful when you send money. As soon as the money is out of your wallet, it's gone forever, and there is no way to get it back. There are no chargebacks and you can't call customer support. Your money is gone.

Triple-check the wallet address before sending. You want to make sure you're sending it to the right address. Also double check the address even if you copy and paste it. There is malicious software out there that can swap your addresses for Ctrl+C/Ctrl+V commands.

Take Care When Using Exchanges

Cryptocurrency exchanges are central points that hackers like to target to steal tokens. They're seen as pots of gold just ripe for the picking, and more than 150 of them have been compromised.

Keep this in mind while using exchanges, and follow the best practices laid out in this book to keep your tokens safe. Do a little research on the exchange you're using to see what security measures it has in place.

Two-factor authentication is critical. You may also consider setting up a secret phrase with your telecom provider to help prevent social engineering. You don't want to be the victim of a SIM card swap. Your phone number doesn't have to be your backup; Google and several other companies also offer a two-factor authentication option (check out the Google Authenticator app).

Finally, just use exchanges to move your funds in and out. Don't use the exchange as a place to store value. Instead, hold significant amounts of crypto in cold storage or in a laminated paper wallet with several copies.

Beware Wi-Fi

If your router wasn't set up correctly, it's possible for someone to see a log of all your activity. Also, when you're on an unsecured or public portal, you may also be exposed to malware. You must assume that the owner of the network can see your activity.

WARNING

Only use trusted Wi-Fi networks and make sure you've changed the password on your router to something as secure as a password. Most Wi-Fi router passwords are set to a factory default of "admin" and can easily be taken over by a third party.

Identify Your Blockchain Dev

Blockchain technology is new, and there just aren't that many people who have a lot of experience when it comes to building blockchain applications.

If you're thinking about hiring a developer to help you with a project, check out her GitHub and see what work she's done before you get started. She may not need to be experienced with blockchain specifically, but if she isn't, she should be a very experienced developer outside of the blockchain world.

There aren't many resources out there yet to help developers when they get stuck. Inexperienced developers may struggle, and at this point most are inexperienced and will take longer to develop your application.

Don't Get Suckered

The blockchain industry as a whole does not have the same protection and security measures that banks and other financial institutions have, and there are not the same laws for your protection and financial welfare. There is no consumer protection and no FDIC bank insurance of funds from the government. If you get robbed or conned, you may not be able to turn to anyone for help.

Also, the industry has had a lot of hype in the last few years without much delivery of things of real value. The year 2016 saw over a thousand new blockchain companies pop up overnight claiming expertise. When you're looking at developing a project and trying to decide if it's worth the investment, it's always a good idea to take a minute and make sure it even makes sense. Ask yourself the following questions:

>> Is there real value generated?

>> Is the value created in the way that benefits you?

>> Why hasn't it been done already?

>> Are there other more tested technologies that could be used to accomplish the same thing with the same efficiency or better?

Blockchain technology holds a lot of promise and power and, as such, should be approached thoughtfully and carefully.

Don't Trade Tokens Unless You Know What You're Doing

Cryptocurrencies are very volatile and will swing wildly in value at any given time and sometimes for no discernable reason. Many of the cryptocurrencies have little depth, and trading large amounts can crash the market value. Working with public blockchains means that you'll likely need to hold some amount of the currency to utilize them.

Don't get caught up in trading the tokens unless you take the time to understand the market well. A good rule of thumb is if you haven't traded traditional assets like stock before, be sure to take extra time to understand cryptocurrency. You need to dive just as deep into it as you would to learn about the stock market before you get started. Consider reading *Cryptocurrency Investing For Dummies* by Kiana Danial (Wiley). If you do choose to trade the tokens and cryptocurrencies, don't forget to report this activity to your accountant. You may need to report your gains or loses on your income tax return.

Chapter **19**

Ten Top Blockchain Projects

New blockchain startups are emerging every day. Entrepreneurs have seen opportunities to capitalize on the very powerful tools blockchains offer to move money faster, secure computer systems, and build digital identities.

In this chapter, I introduce you to some of my favorite projects and companies. After reading this chapter, you'll have an idea of some of the amazing things happening within the blockchain software space. You may even get some ideas about what you could do yourself!

The R3 Consortium

Many banks have invested in building blockchain prototypes — many for Know Your Customer (KYC) requirements for anti-money laundering and prototypes for reducing the cost of exchanging money. They have to overcome several challenges, including the security of private information and the regulatory gray zone of cryptocurrencies.

R3 (www.r3cev.com) is an innovative company that has built a consortium with more than 75 of the world's leading financial institutions to integrate and take advantage of new blockchain technology. R3 is improving cross-border exchange, lowering the cost of auditing, and improving the speed of interbank fund transfer and settlement.

R3's three pillars are as follows:

>> **Financial-grade blockchain:** R3 has developed the base layer technology that supports a global financial institution's needs.

>> **Research and development:** R3 has created a bilateral research center that is testing and creating industry standards for commercial-grade blockchain technology.

>> **Product development:** R3 works in close collaboration with institutions to create products that solve problems up and down the value chain.

R3 has developed a blockchain platform for financial institutions called Corda. Corda is a distributed ledger platform designed to manage and synchronize financial agreements between regulated financial institutions. Unlike most blockchains that broadcast their transactions to the whole network, transactions may execute in parallel, on different nodes, without either node being aware of the other's transactions. The history of the network is on a need-to-know basis.

Key features of Corda include the following:

>> **Controlled access:** Only parties with a legitimate need to know can see the data.

>> **No central controller.**

>> **Regulatory and supervisory observer nodes.**

>> **Validation by parties to the transaction rather than a broader pool of unrelated validators.**

>> **Support for a variety of consensus mechanisms.**

>> **No native cryptocurrency, but now working with Ripples XRP.**

T ZERO: Overstocking the Stock Market

T ZERO is a platform that integrates blockchain technology with existing market processes to reduce settlement time and costs and increase transparency, efficiency, and auditability. T ZERO is able to do this because it's modular and adaptable.

T ZERO is a subsidiary of Overstock.com, focusing on the development and commercialization of fintech-based technologies based on cryptographically secured, decentralized ledgers. Since its inception in October 2014, T ZERO (www.t0.com) has established working commercial blockchain products.

It partnered with Keystone Capital Corporation, an independent broker-dealer located in California to create the first public issuance of blockchain equities. Together they provide brokerage services for users that trade blockchain securities.

Patrick Byrne, Overstock's founder and CEO, led this initiative. The opaque business practices of Wall Street have opened up market opportunities for a clear and trustworthy trading platform where consumers know what they're buying and the costs involved. The SEC declared parent company Overstock.com's S-3 filing effective, giving Overstock.com the ability to issue blockchain shares in a public offering. It also partnered with the Industrial and Commercial of Bank of China (ICBC), the world's largest bank, to test the platform.

Byrne achieves this through Medici, Overstock.com's majority-owned financial technology subsidiary. Medici focuses on applying blockchain technology to solving significant financial transaction problems. Its first initiative is to clean up securities settlement.

Blockstream's Distributed Systems

Blockstream (www.blockstream.com) has an excellent reputation in providing blockchain technologies and has a primary focus on distributed systems. Blockstream offers hardware and software solutions to organizations utilizing blockchain-based networks.

Blockstream Elements is the core software platform of the company and a segment of an open-source project. It offers several resources and a highly productive protocol for blockchain developers.

Blockstream's major field of innovation is in sidechains, which scale the utility of existing blockchains, enhancing their privacy and functionality by adding features like smart contracts and confidential transactions. Sidechains avoid liquidity shortages that many cryptocurrencies experience. Sidechains also permit digital assets to be transferred between different blockchains.

Sidechains make it possible to practically trade company shares on a blockchain without worrying about transaction cost or slow network speeds. Distributed asset management infrastructure can also leverage the Bitcoin network, permitting individuals and organizations to issue different asset classes.

Blockstream also has worked to create the Lightning Network, a system that lets Bitcoin support micropayment without slowing down the network. The Lightning Network support high volumes of small payments using proportional transaction fees and operating very fast. It's developing more Bitcoin Lightning prototypes and creating consensus and interoperability.

MadHive

The MAD Network founded by Tom Bolich and Adam Helfgott aims to create a new way of advertising on the Internet. Given that the Internet was built on things like pay-per-click, and social media marketing and Google and Facebook would not be the powerhouses they are today without advertising, what MadHive is achieving is very interesting. They're building a custom ad engine with blockchain software that allows users to remain private while also giving advertisers better outcomes on several fronts.

TIP

In online marketing, companies looking to find new customers can place online advertisements on web pages that show results from search engine queries that target users search history. An ad engine enables this technology.

As a company, MadHive believes that privacy is a human right; this is different from any other ad engine on the market that needs private consumer information to operate and will do whatever it needs to obtain and link this information.

The MadHive team also believes that marketing industry efforts should never be at odds with the rights of customers. By respecting the privacy of customers, they solve the conflict of interest that marketers have when they need to share data with competitors. Blockchain technology allows for controlled and verifiable sharing of information and is a simple solution to a complex issue. The MAD Network also solves inefficiencies in the online marketing industry by quickly clearing and settling transactions.

The MAD Network is still under active development, but they already have paying customers. To learn more about the work they are doing, check out their website at https://madhive.com/.

Blockdaemon

Blockdaemon is a Docker for blockchain development. Blockdaemon lets you get up and running quickly when you want to build a decentralized application (Dapp), so you don't have to worry as much about understanding each protocol and its native languages — you can just build the app you want. Through the Blockdaemon system, you can orchestrate your blockchain networks across multiple clouds and data centers. They also help you set up testnets and mainnets. If you would like to build a blockchain application or use some blockchain functionality in your app, but you don't want to learn everything about how to build and maintain blockchain software, Blockdaemon is a good alternative. You can learn more about what they're doing at https://blockdaemon.com.

Gemini Dollar and Exchange

Gemini has operated as a cryptocurrency exchange for several years. Founded by the famous Winklevoss twins, it has been conducted differently than other exchanges. Licensed and run out of the state of New York, it has been subject to more oversight. A new and exciting development is the new stable coin Gemini released in 2018 called the Gemini dollar; this is an ER20 token on Ethereum that tracks the value of the U.S. dollar.

You can check out their smart contract at https://etherscan.io/token/0x056Fd409E1d7A124BD7017459dFEa2F387b6d5Cd.

Unlike many other stable coins, Gemini has embraced regulation. The U.S. dollar deposits that back the Gemini dollar balances are audited every month by BPM, LLP, a registered public accounting firm. The accounting firm checks to make sure there is always a one-to-one ratio of U.S. dollars to Gemini dollars. Gemini also went the extra mile and had their code audited for security. Given that smart contracts have proven to be vulnerable to being executed in unexpected ways, this gives a little more assurance that the funds will not disappear.

Decentraland

Decentraland is a virtual reality game that is built on the Ethereum blockchain. It allows users to develop and buy land within their virtual world. You can create, experience, and monetize content and applications. Decentraland is a more extensive platform that enables users to create their games within the context of Decentraland. Within the game, you find things like casinos, music, workshops, and more.

Decentraland started as a small proof of concept in 2015. They distributed ownership of digital real estate. At first, the land was represented as a pixel on a 2D grid. Each pixel had a bit of data that described it and allocated ownership. In late 2017, the Decentraland team started work on a 3D virtual world. It's divided into parcels instead of pixels. The owner of each parcel of land can associate it with a hash reference to a file.

The new 3D virtual space within Decentraland is now called "LAND," and it functions as a token. LAND is a scarce nonfungible digital asset. An Ethereum smart contract enforces the rules of LAND. LAND is divided into parcels that are owned by users and purchased using an in-game currency called "MANA." The Decentraland software development kit (SDK) provides everything you need to build interactive games or static 3D scenes. You can learn more about Decentraland at https://decentraland.org.

TransferWise

TransferWise is a peer-to-peer money transfer service that allows you to move money from one account and currency to another. It matches people's request to move money and exchange currency and supports about 300 currencies at the time of writing. TransferWise is not specifically blockchain, but it may interact with permission blockchains such as Ripple in the future. It offers what it calls a borderless account, which lets you use a MasterCard debit card. So it's easy to move and spend your money wherever you are in the world. TransferWise advertises low conversion fees and zero transaction fees.

Created by two Estonians in 2010, TransferWise has over 4 million customers and helps them transfer more than $4 billion every month. It also has support from industry disrupters like Richard Branson, Max Levchin, and Peter Thiel.

You can learn more about what TransferWise is doing at https://transferwise.com.

Lightning Network

The Lightning Network is a project that started in 2015 to address the capacity issues that the Bitcoin blockchain was having. It's a second layer over the Bitcoin network that takes transaction of the blockchain and it then batches the transactions. Lightning enables you to transfer Bitcoin almost instantly and at a lower cost. Because the operations are "off chain," security is enforced by smart contracts between you and the other party that you're transacting with. The peer-to-peer nature of Lightning means that it can scale to any market demand and exceed the capacity of legacy payment rails.

The Lightning Network also has support across blockchains. This allows you to exchange tokens or cryptocurrency from one blockchain to another. Called *cross-chain atomic swaps*, these transaction use heterogeneous blockchain consensus rules, where each node is equal. The limitation is that the two blockchains must have the same cryptographic hash function.

Learn more about Lightning at https://lightning.network.

Bitcoin Cash

Bitcoin Cash, also known as BCH, is a newer Bitcoin fork that has focused its efforts on increasing transaction speed and lowering transaction costs. The Bitcoin project and its community split in two in 2017. The Bitcoin Cash team focused on making it easy to use Bitcoin on a daily bases as a means of payment for anyone. BCH is a peer-to-peer electronic cash system that is permissionless and decentralized. There are no third parties and no central banks. The underlying Bitcoin Cash protocol takes its place.

You can find Bitcoin Cash on most exchanges with the BCH ticker symbol. And the Bitcoin Cash protocol will never allow there to be more than 21 million BCH coins in existence. You may consider using Bitcoin Cash because you can send money to anyone, anywhere in the world, at any time, any day of the year. The protocol never sleeps. The fees are low, so no transfer is too big or too small. And you never need anyone's permission or approval. Like other cryptocurrencies, you are your bank and you need to take all the same precautions you would with any other digital asset. This also means that no one can seize your money or freeze your account or block your transactions. Learn more at www.bitcoincash.org.

Index

About the Author

Tiana Laurence is a Blockchain pioneer, investor, and startup founder. She is a founder of Factom, Inc., a software company that builds innovative technology within the blockchain space. She loves writing about emerging technologies and helping the average person understand them. Her passion is growing great companies, and she loves helping young aspiring entrepreneurs learn about business and technology. Tiana has a BA in business and leadership from Portland State University.

Dedication

This one is for my sisters. Thank you for all the support and encouragement you gave me as I was writing this book.

Author's Acknowledgments

This book is the product of many people's ideas and work. It would not have been possible without the open and supportive blockchain and cryptocurrency world. I'd like to thank specifically Paul Snow, Peter Kirby, Brian Deery, and David Johnston for the countless hours spent teaching me about blockchain and cryptography. I'd also like to thank Abhi Dobhal, Lawrence Rufrano, Ryan Fugger, Charley Cooper, Alyse Killeen, Jeremy Kandah, Clemens Wan, Greg Wallace, Brian Behlendorf, Amir Chetrit, Casey Lawlor, and Scott Robinson for the direction and guidance in the evolving blockchain space and for taking time out of their busy lives to review and sanity-check my work.

This book also took a lot of editing. I'm not kidding — it really took a lot of editing. My project editor, Elizabeth Kuball, did a great job keeping me on task and on schedule, and Steve Hayes, my executive editor, made the whole book possible. I'd also like to thank Scott Robinson again for his thorough technical review and excellent suggestions and all the other behind-the-scenes people, who did thankless jobs to bring this book about. I'm forever in their debit.

Publisher's Acknowledgments

Acquisitions Editor: Steve Hayes

Project Editor: Elizabeth Kuball

Copy Editor: Elizabeth Kuball

Technical Editor: Scott Robinson

Editorial Assistant: Matthew Lowe

Sr. Editorial Assistant: Cherie Case

Production Editor: Magesh Elangovan

Cover Image: © ismagilov/iStock/ Getty Images Plus

Take dummies with you everywhere you go!

Whether you are excited about e-books, want more from the web, must have your mobile apps, or are swept up in social media, dummies makes everything easier.

Find us online!

Leverage the power

Dummies is the global leader in the reference category and one of the most trusted and highly regarded brands in the world. No longer just focused on books, customers now have access to the dummies content they need in the format they want. Together we'll craft a solution that engages your customers, stands out from the competition, and helps you meet your goals.

Advertising & Sponsorships

Connect with an engaged audience on a powerful multimedia site, and position your message alongside expert how-to content. Dummies.com is a one-stop shop for free, online information and know-how curated by a team of experts.

- Targeted ads
- Video
- Email Marketing
- Microsites
- Sweepstakes sponsorship

20 **MILLION** PAGE VIEWS **EVERY SINGLE MONTH**

15 MILLION **UNIQUE** VISITORS PER MONTH

43% OF ALL VISITORS ACCESS THE SITE **VIA THEIR MOBILE DEVICES**

700,000 NEWSLETTER SUBSCRIPTIONS **TO THE INBOXES OF** *300,000* UNIQUE INDIVIDUALS EVERY WEEK

# of dummies

Custom Publishing

Reach a global audience in any language by creating a solution that will differentiate you from competitors, amplify your message, and encourage customers to make a buying decision.

- Apps
- Books
- eBooks
- Video
- Audio
- Webinars

Brand Licensing & Content

Leverage the strength of the world's most popular reference brand to reach new audiences and channels of distribution.

For more information, visit **dummies.com/biz**

PERSONAL ENRICHMENT

 **Staying Sharp**
9781119187790
USA $26.00
CAN $31.99
UK £19.99

 **Facebook**
Carolyn Abram
9781119179030
USA $21.99
CAN $25.99
UK £16.99

 **Guitar**
Mark Phillips
Jon Chappell
9781119293354
USA $24.99
CAN $29.99
UK £17.99

 **Investing**
Eric Tyson, MBA
9781119293347
USA $22.99
CAN $27.99
UK £16.99

 **Beekeeping**
Howland Blackiston
9781119310068
USA $22.99
CAN $27.99
UK £16.99

 Digital Photography
Julie Adair King
9781119235606
USA $24.99
CAN $29.99
UK £17.99

 **Meditation**
Stephan Bodian
9781119251163
USA $24.99
CAN $29.99
UK £17.99

 **Pregnancy**
9781119235491
USA $26.99
CAN $31.99
UK £19.99

 **Samsung Galaxy S7**
Bill Hughes
9781119279952
USA $24.99
CAN $29.99
UK £17.99

 iPhone
Edward C. Baig
Bob "Dr. Mac" LeVitus
9781119283133
USA $24.99
CAN $29.99
UK £17.99

 **Crocheting**
Karen Manthey
Susan Brittain
9781119287117
USA $24.99
CAN $29.99
UK £16.99

 **Nutrition**
Carol Ann Rinzler
9781119130246
USA $22.99
CAN $27.99
UK £16.99

PROFESSIONAL DEVELOPMENT

 Windows 10
Andy Rathbone
9781119311041
USA $24.99
CAN $29.99
UK £17.99

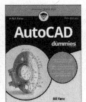 **AutoCAD**
Bill Fane
9781119255796
USA $39.99
CAN $47.99
UK £27.99

 **Excel 2016**
Greg Harvey, PhD
9781119293439
USA $26.99
CAN $31.99
UK £19.99

 **QuickBooks 2017**
9781119281467
USA $26.99
CAN $31.99
UK £19.99

 **macOS Sierra**
Raphael L. Nelson, MBA, CPA, SAS in Tutorials
Bob "Dr. Mac" LeVitus
9781119280651
USA $29.99
CAN $35.99
UK £21.99

 **LinkedIn**
Joel Elad, MBA
9781119251132
USA $24.99
CAN $29.99
UK £17.99

 **Windows 10**
Woody Leonhard
9781119310563
USA $34.00
CAN $41.99
UK £24.99

 **SharePoint 2016**
Rosemarie Withee
Ken Withee
9781119181705
USA $29.99
CAN $35.99
UK £21.99

 **Fundamental Analysis**
Matt Krantz
9781119263593
USA $26.99
CAN $31.99
UK £19.99

 **Networking**
Doug Lowe
9781119257769
USA $29.99
CAN $35.99
UK £21.99

 **Office 2016**
Wallace Wang
9781119293477
USA $26.99
CAN $31.99
UK £19.99

 Office 365
Rosemarie Withee
Ken Withee
Jennifer Reed
9781119265313
USA $24.99
CAN $29.99
UK £17.99

 Salesforce.com
Liz Kao
Jon Paz
9781119239314
USA $29.99
CAN $35.99
UK £21.99

 **Coding**
Nikhil Abraham
9781119293323
USA $29.99
CAN $35.99
UK £21.99

dummies.com

dummies®
A Wiley Brand

Learning Made Easy

ACADEMIC

9781119293576
USA $19.99
CAN $23.99
UK £15.99

9781119293637
USA $19.99
CAN $23.99
UK £15.99

9781119293491
USA $19.99
CAN $23.99
UK £15.99

9781119293460
USA $19.99
CAN $23.99
UK £15.99

9781119293590
USA $19.99
CAN $23.99
UK £15.99

9781119215844
USA $26.99
CAN $31.99
UK £19.99

9781119293378
USA $22.99
CAN $27.99
UK £16.99

9781119293521
USA $19.99
CAN $23.99
UK £15.99

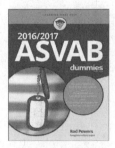

9781119239178
USA $18.99
CAN $22.99
UK £14.99

9781119263883
USA $26.99
CAN $31.99
UK £19.99

Available Everywhere Books Are Sold

dummies.com